# Anchored in His Word

**Devotional Stories for the Journey**

## Charles E. Cravey

In His Steps Publishing

ISBN: 978-1-58535-038-4 (PAPERBACK)

ISBN: 978-1-58535-039-1 (KINDLE)

Library of Congress Catalog Number: 2025904846

Scriptures are from the King James Version of the Bible

Cover by Charles E. Cravey and Book Brush

# Contents

# Introduction

In the vast ocean of life, we often navigate through the unpredictable waters of uncertainty, challenges, and doubt.
Our faith is the compass that guides us, and God's Word is
the anchor that holds us steady.

This book, ***Anchored in His Word: Devotional Stories for the Journey***, is a collection of heartfelt devotional
stories designed to inspire and strengthen your faith. Each
story is a testament to the power of God's love and the
unwavering support He provides in our daily lives.

As you embark on this journey through these pages, may
you find solace in the words of Scripture and the experiences shared by fellow believers. May these stories remind
you that His abiding Word anchors you, and through
Him, you will find the strength and courage to navigate
any obstacle, regardless of the storm.

May this book be a beacon of hope, guiding you towards

a deeper connection with God and a renewed sense of purpose. Embrace each story as a source of encouragement, and let His Word be the steadfast anchor that keeps you grounded in faith.

Welcome to ***Anchored in His Word: Devotional Stories for the Journey***. May this journey be a blessing to you.

Editor: In His Steps Publishing

# Foreword

This book marks the 30th of my career in writing. It all began with the newspaper column, Fruits from the Vineyard, that I wrote in various Georgia newspapers for over 30 years. In Warner Robins, Georgia, while pastoring in that wonderful city, I began a poetry society that met monthly in the local library. I gave the group the name of The Society of American Poets.

Each poet wanted to see their works in print, so I began the arduous process of discovering how to begin a publishing company and how I would print the books. After much study, I began In His Steps Publishing and began publishing our poetry books. That would eventually lead me to compile, edit, and publish thousands of poems from poets across the United States and overseas. I published THE POET'S PEN magazine for twenty years, enabling many of our poets to win awards through the years. Other poetry societies nationally knew and recognized us.

It has all been for the love of God and my devotion to the kingdom of heaven. From those early publishing days, when no traditional publisher would give me the time of day, I began publishing my own books. We have since published over four hundred books for people in various states with much success, and we are immensely proud of each. I design the covers, secure the ISBN numbers, register each book with the Library of Congress, and have the books printed by outsourcing. Our primary goal was to share our faith, and we believe we've done that. Since you are holding and reading one of our books, it tells me we have been successful. God bless you.

The Rev. Dr. Charles E. Cravey, March 2025

https://drcharlescravey.com (To Order Other Books by the Author)

Contact me for further info at: drrev@msn.com or craveyce@gmail.com

# 1

# Baseball's Anchor

A S A YOUNG CHILD, I eagerly anticipated baseball practice, reveling in my love for the sport. During my first year of Little League, my coach recognized my potential and assigned me the role of second baseman. Thriving in this position, I honed my skills and embraced the challenges that came with it. However, fate had other plans for me during our first official game when our catcher got injured. With no prior experience as a catcher, I was called upon to step into the role for the rest of the game.

Struggling to adjust to the unfamiliar gear and obstructed vision caused by the catcher's mask, I found myself in a predicament. Closing my eyes and relying on instinct, I did my best to catch the pitcher's throws. Despite the initial uncertainty and clumsiness, I persevered through the game and eventually emerged as the team's starting catcher. This unexpected turn of events led to me being selected as the catcher for the All-Star teams each year, further solidifying my position on the field and highlighting my determination to adapt and succeed.

In the game of baseball, the catcher plays a crucial role as the team anchor. While a team may go through several pitchers throughout a game, the catcher remains the one solid position player that provides stability and consistency in the field. The catcher handles not only catching pitches from the pitcher, but also calling the pitches, managing the defense, and controlling the pace of the game.

People often see the catcher as the team leader, guiding and supporting the pitchers and other players to perform at their best. Overall, the catcher's presence in the field is essential for the success and cohesion of the team.

As a dedicated catcher, I took my position in the field with a keen sense of responsibility and leadership. Guiding my team to success was a fulfilling challenge I embraced wholeheartedly. Through practice and determination, I honed my skills in throwing out base runners at both second and third base, highlighting my accuracy and speed.

I developed a strategic edge by seizing opportunities to catch opposing players off guard, occasionally surprising a runner on first base with a quick throw. This element of surprise fueled my passion for the game, as I found joy in outsmarting my opponents and contributing to my team's victories.

The successful Johnny Bench was my idol. To me, he was the best in the game and anchored the Cincinnati Reds each season for several years of successful baseball. His exceptional skills as a catcher, powerful hitting, and leadership on and off the field made him a legendary figure in baseball history. Johnny Bench's impact went beyond his individual accomplishments, as he inspired countless fans and aspiring players with his dedication and passion for the game. His legacy continues to resonate in the world of baseball, serving as a timeless example of excellence and fair play.

They picked me as the team catcher on my first day of high school. All my fellow teammates chose me because I had impressed them back in the Little League and Pony League. I took immense pride in that and played my heart out during the season, earning the player of the year award at our little banquet as the season ended.

An anchor holds something down, as it keeps a vessel secured in place by gripping the seabed. Shipbuilders typically make this essential maritime tool from heavy metal and attach it to a strong chain or rope. Anchors come in distinct designs, such as fluke, plow, and mushroom, each suited for different seabeds and weather. When a ship drops anchor, it relies on this crucial equipment to prevent drifting and ensure stability while docked or at sea.

As an anchor for many years in baseball, I took my job seriously. I played a crucial role in directing the outfielders to shift positions based on the tendencies of specific batters. By analyzing where a batter was most likely to hit the ball, I provided valuable insights to my teammates, who relied on me to guide their defensive positioning.

The pitchers on our team trusted me to make strategic decisions on which type of pitch to throw—whether it be a curveball, slider, or fast ball. My expertise and quick decision-making skills were essential in ensuring the success of our team in the field.

I received a new catcher's mitt and cleats from my Little League coach my first year. He told me to play my heart out, and I did, for years to come. Work was the only thing that eventually took me away from baseball. My ambition was to follow in Johnny Bench's footsteps. However, life's demands and the need to earn a living forced me to abandon the only sport I ever loved.

I enjoyed being the team anchor and took that position seriously. Players respected me for that and would lean on me to direct them, whether it was in the field or at the plate.

I later became the anchor for my family when Renee and I had our first child and then a second one. I took the position again just as seriously as I had catching in baseball. And then, called to preach, I took the anchor of various churches I pastored across South Georgia, leading churches forward in faith and closer to God. I would anchor marriages, funerals, baptisms, and ceremonies as a pastor. People would trust me to do the right thing and call the plays.

In this journey of faith and leadership, I transitioned from being a dedicated family anchor to a steadfast pastor, guiding congregations in their spiritual journeys. As a pastor, I took on the responsibility of leading churches in South Georgia, fostering a sense of community and faith among the members. Whether anchoring marriages, conducting funerals, or performing baptisms, I strived to bring people closer to God and provide them with the support and guidance they needed in their spiritual lives. My dedication to right action and integrity earned the community's trust, thus enabling me to effectively make calls and positively impact the lives of those around me.

An anchor holds!

# 2

# Saint Paul and the Oyster

H ARRY EMERSON FOSDICK ONCE said, "The most extraordinary thing about the oyster is this: irritations get into his shell. He does not like them. But when he cannot get rid of them, he uses the irritation to do the loveliest thing an oyster ever has a chance to do. If there are irritations in our lives today, there is only one prescription: make a pearl."

This profound metaphor encourages us to transform our challenges into opportunities for growth and beauty. Just as the oyster turns a grain of sand into a precious pearl, we, too, can take life's irritations and hardships and use them to create something meaningful. This approach not only helps us cope with difficulties but also empowers us to find hidden strengths and talents within ourselves. Embracing this perspective can lead to personal development, resilience, and a more fulfilling life. Remember, every irritation is an opportunity to create your own unique pearl.

The apostle Paul had his "thorn in the flesh." This metaphorical thorn, though a source of discomfort, became a catalyst for deeper insight and reliance on inner strength. Paul's experience teaches us that even persistent challenges can serve a greater purpose, fostering humility and resilience. By embracing our own "thorns," we can develop a more profound understanding of ourselves and cultivate a compassionate perspective towards others facing their own struggles. Life's trials, like those faced by the oyster and Paul, can refine us. They offer opportunities for growth and a richer life.

In this journey, it's essential to remember that growth often comes from unexpected places. Challenges and obstacles, much like the oyster's irritants or Paul's thorn, are not merely disruptions but invitations to dig deeper. They encourage us to pause, reflect, and renew our perspective. These moments of introspection can lead to revelations about our values, priorities, and the direction we wish to take.

By sharing our stories of transformation, we inspire others to view their own challenges as opportunities for growth. When we openly discuss our struggles and the pearls we create from them, we foster a sense of community and support. This shared understanding helps to build connections, strengthen relationships, and cultivate collective resilience.

In the end, the process of turning life's irritations into pearls is a testament to the human spirit's ability to adapt and thrive. It is a celebration of our capacity to find light in darkness and beauty in the most unlikely of places. So, let us embrace our challenges with courage and creativity, knowing that each one holds the potential to lead us to a brighter, more meaningful future.

For this reason, I espouse the idea that Paul's thorn became his anchor. It grounded him, providing a constant reminder of his humanity and the necessity of humility. Paul's hardship became his foundation. He used it to deepen his faith and self-understanding and to grow in his comprehension of the world. This anchoring effect can be transformative, offering stability amid life's tumultuous seas.

Just as an anchor provides a vessel with security and steadiness, so too can our challenges and irritations stabilize us. They can keep us focused on what truly matters, reminding us of our values and the strength we possess to navigate through adversity. By accepting and integrating these experiences into our lives, we not only learn to persevere, but also gain clarity and purpose.

In embracing our own "anchors," we create a solid base from which we can explore new horizons with confidence and curiosity. These anchors do not bind us; instead, they provide the assurance we need to venture forth, knowing that we have the inner resources to rise above any storm. So, let us view our challenges not as burdens, but as anchors that keep us true to ourselves and guide us towards a more authentic and enriched existence.

Let me share a personal anecdote with you about Paul's thorn and the oyster's pearl.

I once faced a situation that seemed insurmountable. It was a time of notable change and uncertainty in my life, and I felt as though I was constantly battling against unseen forces. The stress and pressure felt like an ever-present thorn, a constant reminder of my vulnerabilities and limitations.

At first, I resisted, trying to push the discomfort away. But then, inspired by the metaphor of the oyster and Paul's own journey, I embraced this challenge head-on. I saw it not as an obstacle, but as an opportunity for growth. Much like the oyster with its grain of sand, I worked with the irritation, slowly transforming it into something valuable.

Throughout this process, I discovered new strengths within myself that I hadn't known existed. I learned the importance of patience and perseverance, and I found a renewed sense of purpose. This experience became my pearl—a testament to resilience and the power of transformation.

By sharing my story, I hope to encourage others to view their difficulties through a similar lens. Each challenge is a chance to dig deeper, to explore our inner resources, and to emerge stronger and wiser. Just as the oyster and Paul found beauty in their struggles, so, too, can we find our own pearls in life's adversities.

### Reflection on Pearls and Thorns in the Flesh

Pearls and thorns in the flesh are symbolic representations of experiences or aspects of ourselves that hold significance in our lives. They come in various forms, each serving a unique purpose in shaping our identities and journeys. This document explores the duality of pearls and thorns in the flesh, highlighting their impact on personal growth and self-discovery.

Pearls, often associated with beauty, purity, and wisdom, represent moments of joy, success, and enlightenment in our lives. They are like treasures that we cherish, reminding us of the valuable lessons learned and the growth achieved through positive experiences. Moments of triumph, love, and connection with others produce pearls that shine as beacons in the darkness.

Thorns in the flesh symbolize challenges, pain, and struggles that we encounter along our journeys. They can manifest as obstacles, failures, or emotional wounds that test our resilience and character. While thorns may cause discomfort and hardship, they also offer opportunities for introspection, healing, and transformation. Embracing our thorns in the flesh allows us to confront our vulnerabilities, confront our vulnerabilities, and cultivate resilience in the face of adversity.

In conclusion, both pearls and thorns in the flesh play vital roles in shaping who we are and who we are becoming. Both pearls and thorns contribute to our growth, understanding, and evolution, as intertwined aspects of the human experience. By acknowledging and embracing the duality of pearls and thorns in the flesh, we can navigate life's complexities with grace, gratitude, and resilience.

# 3

# The Beacon of Hope

THE TEMPEST RAVAGED THE quaint coastal hamlet of Bert's Landing with an untamed fury. The winds wailed a sorrowful symphony as waves crashed on the shore, inundating streets and sweeping away anything not firmly anchored. Amidst the tumult, a mysterious figure emerged—a cloaked silhouette navigating the deluge, cradling an enigmatic object swathed in fabric. They made their way to the church perched upon the hill, its steeple just a ghostly outline through the cascading torrents.

Within the sanctuary, the townsfolk clustered closely, yearning for solace. Clara, the youthful minister of the village, endeavored to soothe their spirits, even as her own faith lay weary, much like the weathered walls that surrounded them. Days of relentless storms had passed, and the desolation reflected in the eyes of the people echoed the surging tides beyond.

The stranger heaved open the weighty church doors, drenched to the core. Without uttering a word, they unfurled their bundle, unveiling a magnificently adorned anchor. Its metal shimmered, undeterred by the tempest, etched with intricate designs that appeared to shimmer softly.

Clara advanced with trepidation, her voice a whisper on the air. "Who are you? And what brings you to this sacred place with an anchor?"

The stranger's voice flowed like a gentle stream, calm and assured. "I have come to remind you of what it means to be anchored—not merely to the earth, but to hope itself. This is no ordinary anchor; it embodies the strength of those who believe, even as the tempest howls."

A ripple of confusion swept through the townspeople. Clara fixed her gaze upon the anchor, shadows of doubt swirling in her mind. "Hope won't halt the waters from rising," she replied, frustration lacing her tone. "What value is faith when all we've crafted is being swept away?"

The stranger fixed her with a steady gaze. "Faith is not about avoiding the storm—it's about finding the strength to endure it. Did not the psalmist write, 'God is our refuge and strength, a very present help in trouble. Therefore, will not we fear, though the earth be removed, and though the mountains be carried into the midst of the sea'."(Psalm 46:1–2).

Clara felt her breath catch. The verse stirred something deep within her, a flicker of the conviction she'd once carried with ease. The stranger placed the anchor at the foot of the altar and spoke again. "This anchor does not calm the seas, but it steadies the soul. With it, you can rebuild—not just what was lost, but something stronger, rooted in faith."

As the storm howled through the night, the anchor glowed softly, its light illuminating the faces of the weary townsfolk. One by one, they came forward, placing their hands on it as if drawn to its warmth. Each touch infused them with a sense of peace, a reminder that they were not alone in their struggle.

A muted determination spread among them, a shared understanding that their true strength lay not in the absence of adversity but in their unified resolve to face it together. Clara, now emboldened by the stranger's words and the palpable energy emanating from the anchor, spoke with renewed purpose.

"The storm tests us, but it also reveals who we are and what we can become," she declared, her voice unwavering. "Don't let our losses daunt us; let's be inspired by what we can rebuild."

As the night wore on, the townspeople huddled close, exchanging stories, and comforting one another. The anchor's glow was a beacon in the dim sanctuary, a testament to their collective spirit. With each passing moment, the fear that had gripped their hearts loosened its hold.

Outside, the tempest continued its wild dance, yet inside, a quiet strength blossomed. The stranger, watching from the shadows, nodded in silent approval before slipping away unnoticed, leaving the anchor as a gift—a legacy of hope and resilience.

As dawn painted the sky in hues of hope, the storm relinquished its wrath, and the first golden rays of sunlight pierced through the lingering clouds. The townspeople emerged from their sanctuary, eyes squinting against the brilliance, their hearts buoyed, and their spirits unyielding. With Clara at the forefront, they embarked on the sacred mission of rejuvenating their cherished village, every stride illuminated by the enduring spark of hope ignited by the mysterious stranger.

Clara beheld in wonder how the anchor transformed into a beacon—not merely a means of salvation from the tempest but a testament to their resilience amidst it. Empowered, she stood before her congregation, her voice resonating with newfound strength. "Let this anchor remind you that no storm can uproot what hope anchors." *'Which hope we have as an anchor of the soul, both sure and steadfast, and which entereth into that within the veil."* (Hebrews 6:19, NIV). "Together, we shall endure this trial and emerge even stronger."

As morning unfurled its wings, the storm had calmed. The town bore the scars of the tumult, yet its people stood unbroken. Guided by Clara, they set forth to rebuild, nurturing the radiant glow of the anchor deep within their hearts. Though the stranger had vanished into the ether, the anchor remained—a steadfast symbol of the fortitude they had unearthed within themselves and their unwavering faith.

# 4

# Hope's Hearth

FTER THE FIRE THAT destroyed their beloved bakery, William and Elisa Pittman grappled with moments of overwhelming doubt. The devastating loss not only robbed them of their livelihood but also cast a shadow of uncertainty over their children's future. Carlie, a teenager with aspirations of attending art school, and Evan, a young elementary school student, looked to their parents for stability as they navigated their own fears and anxieties.

One particularly cold evening, the Pittman family huddled around a single borrowed heater in the church hall, seeking solace in each other's presence. It was during this trying time that Elisa offered words of reassurance, reminding her family that while they may have lost their physical home, their faith remained a steadfast shelter. In a touching moment of unity, they turned to their worn family Bible and found comfort in the words of Psalm 46:1: "God is our refuge and strength, an ever-present help in trouble." These timeless words breathed new life into their weary hearts, reminding them that even in the face of adversity, they were not alone.

As the Pittman family embarked on the challenging journey of rebuilding their lives in the fire's aftermath, they clung to their faith and the unwavering support of their community. Through shared prayers, acts of kindness, and a resilient spirit, they saw glimmers of hope amidst the ashes. The Pittman's story serves as a poignant reminder of the power of faith, family, and resilience in overcoming life's greatest trials. William, despite his health challenges, refused to let despair take hold. He said, "We may seem broken, but we will not let ourselves become defeated."

Faced with adversity, the Pittman family found strength in their faith, drawing on their beliefs to navigate the uncertainties of rebuilding their lives. As they grappled with the aftermath of a devastating event that left their home in ruins, the Pittman's turned to their faith as a guiding light in the darkness. The community, recognizing the family's plight, rallied around them, offering prayers, practical assistance, and emotional support. This outpouring of compassion and solidarity displayed the power of unity in times of crisis, demonstrating how a community can come together to uplift and support its members in their time of need.

Although faced with insurmountable challenges and setbacks, the Pittman's remained steadfast in their determination to rise above the ashes. With unwavering resolve and the unwavering support of their community, the family embarked on the arduous journey of rebuilding their home and their lives. Through perseverance, resilience, and a deep-rooted faith, the Pittman's emerged stronger and more united than ever before, a testament to the power of belief, community, and the human spirit in overcoming adversity.

William's unshakable resolve and refusal to succumb to despair inspired those around him, demonstrating the resilience that can emerge from even the darkest of circumstances. His words echoed a sentiment of hope and determination that resonated with all who knew the Pittman family. Their story exemplified the strength of faith, the importance of family, and the resilience needed to overcome life's challenges.

The Pittman family's journey serves as a powerful reminder of the human spirit's capacity to persevere in the face of adversity. William's steadfast determination not only uplifted his own spirits but also became a beacon of hope for others. His ability to find strength amid challenges highlighted the transformative power of resilience.

William Pittman, a devoted husband and father of two, faced numerous obstacles throughout his life. From financial struggles to health issues, William encountered setbacks that would have discouraged many. However, instead of allowing these challenges to defeat him, William confronted them head-on with a tenacious spirit.

Despite the adversity he faced, William remained steadfast in his commitment to his family. His unshakable dedication to providing for his loved ones and creating a better future for them fueled his determination to overcome any obstacle that came his way. Through his actions, William inspired not only his family but also those around him to never lose hope in the face of adversity.

In the end, William Pittman's story is a testament to the resilience of the human spirit. His ability to find strength and hope amid challenges serves as a powerful example of how determination can lead to triumph. The Pittman family's journey shows that determination, resilience, and a positive outlook can overcome even the most daunting obstacles.

Their story highlights the importance of faith as a guiding force during trying times. The Pittman's leaned on their beliefs to navigate through the storm, finding solace and courage in their faith. Their unwavering trust in a higher power provided them with the resilience needed to weather life's toughest moments.

Throughout the Pittman family's journey, their strong bonds served as a source of steadfast support and comfort during times of trials and challenges. The unity and love shared among family members created a solid foundation of strength that enabled them to confront adversity with resilience and determination. As they stood together, united in their commitment to overcome obstacles, the power of their family ties became clear in their ability to face hardships as a cohesive and unbreakable unit.

The Pittman family's story is a testament to the resilience, faith, and unity that can help individuals triumph over life's challenges. William's inspiring resolve and the family's determined spirit serve as a reminder of the boundless strength that can emerge from even the darkest of circumstances. Their story is a beacon of hope, demonstrating that with faith, family support, and resolute determination, one can overcome any obstacle that comes their way.

Amid her own challenging circumstances, Elisa's life took a significant turn when she crossed paths with Sharon, a compassionate woman with a heart of gold. Their serendipitous meeting at the local soup kitchen proved to be a pivotal moment for Elisa. Sharon, who had once experienced homelessness herself, shared her inspiring story of resilience and redemption with Elisa. This powerful encounter sparked a deep connection between the two women, leading to the formation of a profound friendship.

United by a shared desire to make a positive impact in their community, Elisa and Sharon embarked on a mission to provide support and solace to those in need. Together, they started weekly gatherings that served as a safe space for individuals to open about their struggles, offer each other support, and nurture a sense of hope. Through these gatherings, a sense of camaraderie and understanding blossomed among the participants, creating a network of mutual aid and solidarity.

As Elisa and Sharon continued to devote their time and energy to this noble cause, they witnessed firsthand the transformative power of empathy and connection. Through their intense dedication and compassionate spirit, they not only brought light into the lives of others but also experienced profound personal growth and fulfillment. The bond forged between Elisa and Sharon exemplified the beauty of human kindness and the enduring impact of reaching out a helping hand to those in need.

In a small corner of the bustling city, William saw an opportunity to transform his bread-making workshops into something more profound than just a skill-sharing class. With a vision to impart life lessons on resilience and faith, William turned each workshop onto a platform for personal growth and introspection. Through the art of bread-making, he weaved a narrative of hope and perseverance for his participants.

Every loaf of bread crafted in William's workshops became more than just a baked good - it became a powerful metaphor for life's journey. "Just as dough needs time to rise, so do we," William would often say, encouraging his students to embrace the process of growth and change. The warmth emanating from the freshly baked bread served as a tangible symbol of the hope and unity they were fostering together.

William's workshops were not just about mastering the art of baking; they were a transformative experience that left a lasting impact on all who attended. Through his teachings and the simple act of making bread, William instilled a sense of resilience and faith in his participants, empowering them to face life's challenges with courage and optimism.

Carlie found her own unique way to give back by painting uplifting murals in temporary shelters around town. With donated art supplies, she transformed cold walls into vibrant reminders of renewal. One of her murals depicted a phoenix rising from the ashes, serving as a tribute to her family's journey. Through her creative talent and generosity, Carlie brought hope and inspiration to those in need.

Evan, despite his youthful age, started collecting and distributing care packages to other children in need, adding personal notes like, "Stay strong, you are not alone."

The Pittman family's enduring faith in the face of adversity served as a beacon of inspiration for their neighbors. Witnessing their resilience, a small group of towns-folk came together to organize a community potluck to raise funds for the family. What began as a modest effort quickly gained momentum and evolved into a town-wide initiative, with individuals generously contributing their time, money, and resources to support the cause.

Hundreds of faces, all sharing a common goal of helping rebuild the Pittman family's beloved bakery, deeply moved the family as they gathered for the potluck that night. The overwhelming display of unity and support highlighted the power of community coming together in times of need.

When the bakery reopened as "Hope's Hearth," it transformed into more than just a business - it became a beacon of hope and a center of community engagement. Photos and murals depicting William and Elisa's journey and values adorned the bakery walls. The bakery desig-nated a corner as a "Hope Board," where patrons could leave messages of encouragement or share resources for those in need. William and Elisa started a "pay-it-forward" program, ensuring that everyone who entered the bakery would never leave hungry, regardless of their ability to pay.

Over the years, the impact of Hope's Hearth extended beyond its physical location. Carlie's murals, originally displayed in the bakery, had become recognizable landmarks throughout the town. Evan, inspired by the kindness his family received at Hope's Hearth, established a foundation to support children in crisis. The Pittman's, through their unshakable faith and perseverance, continued to spread their message of hope and community, serving as a reminder that amidst life's challenges, the support of faith and a strong community can lead to the creation of something even more significant than what was lost.

The Pittman's were now anchored completely in their community. What can you give back today?

—◦❖◦—

# 5

# Tethered to the Stars

MISSION LOG: CAPTAIN OMNE Crow's Exploration of Desolate Planet XJ-27

The desolate planet XJ-27 presented a stark landscape, with vast stretches of blue-hued rock that shimmered faintly under the twin suns. Captain Omne Crow embarked on a routine survey mission to this uninhabited world, securing her tether to the spacecraft's anchor point before venturing out to explore the terrain. However, the mission took an unexpected turn when Omne detected a signal—a rhythmic, purposeful sound that seemed almost musical amidst the static of her communications device.

"Command, are you picking this up?" Omne's voice conveyed a mix of excitement and unease as she sought confirmation of the mysterious signal. The reply came back distorted, showing the vast distance between her and the relay station. "Negative, Captain. We're not detecting anything unusual. Stay tethered," the response advised, urging caution in the unknown's face.

As Omne pondered the source of the enigmatic signal echoing across the desolate planet, she knew that her exploration of XJ-27 was far from over. The mystery of the musical transmission beckoned, promising an adventure beyond the confines of routine survey missions. Omne's hand instinctively brushed the tether at her waist. The anchor cable stretched back toward her ship, the *Stellar Dawn*, its sturdy presence a reminder of the dangers of venturing too far. But the signal—it wasn't coming from her ship. It was emanating from somewhere deep within the jagged ravine ahead, pulsing like the heartbeat of the planet itself. She hesitated. The protocol was clear: do not sever the tether. But as the signal grew stronger, it seemed to speak to her in a way she couldn't explain. It wasn't just sound—it was a pull, a longing that resonated in her very bones.

As Omne stood at the precipice of the ravine, the alien landscape of XJ-27 sprawled before her. An eerie light bathed the rugged terrain, casting long shadows that seemed to dance to the rhythm of the mysterious signal.

The air was thick with anticipation, a palpable sense of the unknown that sent shivers down Omne's spine.

With a deep breath, Omne decided. Ignoring the cautionary voice in her mind, she unclipped the tether from her belt and took a tentative step forward. The ground beneath her feet was uneven, the rocks sharp and unforgiving. But the pull of the signal was undeniable, drawing her deeper into the ravine with each passing moment.

As she ventured further into the heart of the canyon, the signal grew louder, filling her ears with its haunting melody. It was unlike anything she had ever heard, a symphony of alien notes that seemed to address to her soul. Omne felt a surge of adrenaline as she pressed on, the allure of the unknown overpowering any lingering doubts.

The ravine's walls closed in on her, narrowing the path until Omne had to squeeze through a narrow crevice. As she emerged on the other side, she found herself in a vast cavern, illuminated by a soft, pulsating light. And there, at the center of the chamber, was the source of the signal.

It was a strange, otherworldly device, its intricate design a testament to a technology far beyond anything Omne had encountered before. As she approached, the device hummed with energy, the air around it crackling with an unseen power. Omne reached out a trembling hand, her fingers brushing against the smooth surface of the artifact.

And in that moment, as the signal enveloped her completely, Omne knew that her life would never be the same.

"Omne, stay anchored," she whispered to herself, gripping the tether tightly.

The signal flared, louder, more urgently. Her heart raced as the strange melody seemed to promise something—answers, discovery, or a connection to the vast unknown. Against every protocol drilled into her, Omne made a choice. She unhooked the tether.

As she did that, the world around her seemed to shift. The air thickened, vibrating with energy. The rocky terrain glowed, and the signal transformed into something unmistakably alive. It wasn't a sound—it was a voice. Fragmented and alien, yet achingly familiar.

"Why have you come?" the voice asked, resonating in her mind rather than her ears.

"I—" Omne struggled to find words. "I came here because something drew me here. What are you?"

The air shimmered, and before her appeared a being of pure light, its form ever-changing, like liquid starlight. "We are the Tethered. Bound to this place by a choice made long ago. And now you are here, untethered, seeking what lies beyond."

Omne's mind raced. The legends of ancient civilizations sacrificing their freedom to harness the energy of dying stars came flooding back. Was this what she had found? Beings who had become one with the cosmos, but at the cost of their individuality.

"Why me?" Omne asked, her voice trembling. "Why call to me?"

The being's light dimmed, mournfully. "Because you, too, are tethered—not by a cable, but by the weight of your past. You carry it with you, fearing to let it go." Omne's breath caught in her throat. Memories of the loss she had carried for years surfaced—the crew she had failed to save, the guilt that had kept her anchored to the past.

"What must I do?" she asked.

### A Journey of Discovery

Omne stood on the rocky surface of the mysterious planet, feeling the weight of her grief heavy upon her. Suddenly, a being approached her, extending a tendril of light that penetrated her very soul. Feeling the light touch her, she experienced profound release; her burdens floated away into the ether.

"Release what binds you," the voice echoed in her mind. "Only then can you truly explore the stars."

As the light faded, Omne found herself back at her ship, the *Stellar Dawn*, her tether reattached. The planet was now silent, devoid of the signal that had drawn her there. Yet, within herself, Omne felt a newfound lightness and freedom that she had been missing for years.

With a sense of gratitude, Omne boarded her ship, casting one last glance at the planet she had visited. She whispered a muted thank-you, realizing that her genuine discovery had not been in the stars, but deep within herself.

## A Journey Through Guilt and Redemption

As the light of the alien being faded, Omne found herself alone once more, tethered to the cable and standing on the desolate planet's surface. Yet, she wasn't the same. The voice and the being's words echoed within her— "Release what binds you. Only then can you truly explore the stars." Her thoughts swirled like the cosmic storms she had once charted on distant worlds.

Omne had spent years trying to bury her guilt—shoving it into the darkest corners of her mind. Her mistakes haunted her memory. Losing her crewmates during a rescue mission gone awry wasn't just a professional failure;

it was a personal one. She had promised them safety, and the stars had betrayed her. Or it was herself she could no longer trust.

As she stood on the alien planet, Omne realized that the path to redemption was not through avoiding her past, but by confronting it. The alien being's words had ignited a spark within her, urging her to break free from the chains of guilt and self-doubt. With each step she took on the unfamiliar terrain, she felt a sense of liberation washing over her.

The stars above seemed to shimmer with newfound meaning, beckoning her to embrace the unknown and embark on a journey of self-discovery. Omne knew that the road ahead would be challenging, filled with obstacles and uncertainties. But for the first time in years, she felt a glimmer of hope shining in the vast darkness of space.

Omne gazed at the vast sky. She vowed to honor her fallen comrades by forging an alternative path among the stars, driven by courage, resilience, and the conquering of her inner demons. The alien being's message had sparked a transformation within her, setting her on a course towards redemption and a newfound sense of purpose in the cosmos.

## The Weight of Survival

As she trudged back toward the *Stellar Dawn*, the heaviness of her boots defied gravity, a tangible reminder of the burdens she carried within. Each step was a painful journey through memories of faces she had loved and lost during the ill-fated mission. Commander Grant's steady guidance, Lina's mechanical prowess, and Anders' selfless sacrifice haunted her with every flash of their images. Anders, her closest friend, had given her his last breath, a selfless act that still echoed in her mind: "You'll make it out. You must." The survivor's guilt she carried was a relentless weight on her soul, constricting her dreams and suffocating her joy. Despite physically escaping the mission, she remained trapped in a limbo, disconnected from her crew, and most importantly, from herself.

## The Transformative Power of Grief

As she reached the edge of the ravine, Omne glanced back toward the glow she had seen earlier. The being had called her guilt a tether, but it had also called it a weight she could transform. How could something so heavy, so suffocating, become a source of strength? She sat on the rocky ledge, her hands trembling. For the first time in years, Omne allowed herself to cry—truly cry, for all she had endured, for the lives lost, for the person she had once been. The vast sky above twinkled with stars that seemed closer now, as though leaning in to witness her grief. And then she felt it—a faint warmth in her chest. Not comfort exactly, but recognition. It was as if the light of those stars wasn't judging her but holding her burden alongside her. She remembered how Anders used to point to the constellations and say, "We're all made of the same stuff. Don't forget that Omne. It means you're never alone."

In that moment of vulnerability, Omne's emotions cascaded like a tumultuous river breaking through a dam. Each tear that fell carried with it a fragment of her pain, releasing a little bit of the weight that had burdened her for so long. The night air enveloped her, offering a gentle embrace that whispered of understanding and acceptance. The stars above seemed to twinkle in unison with her tears, creating a symphony of sorrow and solace.

As Omne gazed up at the celestial expanse, a sense of connection washed over her. She realized that her grief, rather than being a shackle, could be a catalyst for transformation. It was a reminder of her humanity, her capacity to feel deeply and to carry the burdens of her past. The words of the being echoed in her mind, urging her to embrace her pain as a part of her journey, a steppingstone toward healing and growth.

With a newfound resolve, Omne wiped away her tears and stood up, feeling a renewed sense of purpose coursing through her veins. The stars continued to watch over her, their silent presence a reminder that even in the darkest moments, there was a glimmer of hope. And as she turned away from the ravine, Omne carried with her not just her grief, but also the strength and resilience that came from confronting it head-on.

With a deep breath, Omne rose to her feet on the deck of the *Stellar Dawn*. Her tether to the ship was still secure, but this time, it didn't feel like a chain. It was a connection, a reminder that the past didn't have to trap her—it could guide her, like a star chart etched across her soul. She touched the cable and whispered, "I'm ready."

When she returned to the *Stellar Dawn*, she felt something she hadn't in years—a lightness, an openness to whatever lay ahead. The ship's interior, once a hollow shell, now felt like a vessel of possibility. As she powered up the engines, the signal that had called her earlier pulsed faintly in the distance, not as a lure, but as a reminder. It wasn't the planet or the stars that had given her freedom;

it was the act of confronting herself. For the first time, a muted, luminous hope filled the void inside her.

Omne charted her course and looked out at the vast expanse before her. Her guilt had held her captive, but now a belief that she could carry both her pain and her purpose into the stars held her fast. The journey ahead was not just about exploring the universe, but also about exploring the depths of her own being. As the engines hummed to life, Omne set sail into the unknown, ready to embrace the challenges and revelations that awaited her on her path of self-discovery.

# 6

# Anchor Metaphors

NCHORS ARE RICH IN metaphorical potential, offering layers of meaning. Here are a few I've gleaned from my studies.

**An Anchor is a Lifeline:**

An anchor serves as a lifeline, symbolizing a vital connection to safety and security. Just as a lifeline prevents someone from drifting too far in uncertain waters, an anchor provides stability and protection against the unpredictable forces of nature. The weight and strength of an anchor represent resilience and steadfastness, anchoring us in times of turbulence and uncertainty. This symbolism highlights the importance of staying grounded and connected to our roots, even in the face of challenges or adversity. An anchor is not merely a tool for navigation but a powerful metaphor for the essential role of safety and stability in our lives.

**A Guiding Constant:**

In the journey of life, we often navigate through turbulent waters, facing unexpected challenges and uncertainties. In such moments, having a guiding constant can provide us with the stability and direction we need to stay true to ourselves and our values. We can liken this guiding constant to an anchor, a moral compass, or a core value that keeps us steady amidst the chaotic currents of life.

Just like an anchor holds a ship steady amid a storm, our guiding constant serves as a grounding force that helps us maintain our course when faced with adversity. It provides us with a sense of purpose and clarity, guiding our decisions and actions in alignment with our beliefs and principles. A moral compass guides us through life's challenges and temptations. It also helps us stay true to ourselves.

Having a guiding constant is essential for staying anchored in our values and beliefs, especially in times of uncertainty and chaos. By cultivating and nurturing this moral compass, we can find strength, resilience, and a sense of direction that will help us weather any storm that comes our way. Let us strive to identify and uphold our guiding constant, for it is the beacon that will lead us towards a life of purpose, integrity, and fulfillment.

**Holding Fast in a Storm:**

In times of adversity and challenges, the anchor symbolizes resilience and unwavering faith. Just as an anchor keeps a ship steady during a storm, embodying the qualities of the anchor allows individuals to stay rooted and strong amidst personal or spiritual turmoil. This metaphor serves as a reminder to hold fast to one's beliefs and values, even when faced with turbulent circumstances. By drawing strength from the symbolism of the anchor, individuals can navigate through life's storms with determination and steadfastness.

**A Steadying Force in Relationships:**

In any relationship, trust and loyalty serve as a steadying force, providing a solid foundation that holds everything together. When individuals trust each other, they feel secure and confident in their connection. This trust enables them to be vulnerable, knowing that their partner will support and understand them. Loyalty further reinforces this foundation by demonstrating commitment and dedication to the relationship. Together, trust and loyalty create a sense of stability and assurance, allowing relationships to weather challenges and grow stronger. These qualities deepen bonds and sustain connections, making trust and loyalty essential pillars in any successful relationship.

**A Weight That Grounds:**

Anchors serve as a powerful symbol of stability and grounding. They are not only essential for sustaining objects in water but also hold deep metaphorical meanings. While anchors provide stability, they can also represent burdens or responsibilities that keep us grounded. However, just as one must carefully balance a physical anchor for it to serve its purpose effectively, we must also carefully balance the burdens and responsibilities we carry in life.

People commonly use anchors in maritime settings to keep ships in place and prevent them from drifting aimlessly. This function of anchors parallels the way responsibilities and obligations can ground us in our daily lives.

While these responsibilities provide structure and stability, they can also feel like a weight holding us down. Finding the right balance between being grounded and feeling burdened is crucial for maintaining a healthy and fulfilling life.

Anchors symbolize the dual nature of responsibilities and burdens in our lives. They serve as a reminder of the importance of finding a balance between stability and freedom, between being grounded and feeling weighed down. By acknowledging the role of anchors in our lives, we can strive to navigate the challenges of balancing our responsibilities while also allowing ourselves the space to grow and thrive.

**A Point of Rest:**

Just as an anchor allows a vessel to pause and rest, it can be a metaphor for moments of stillness and reflection in life's journey. In times of chaos and uncertainty, finding a point of rest can provide a sense of grounding and peace. Moments of stillness are like anchors in a storm. They help us gather our thoughts, reflect, and prepare for what's ahead. Embracing these points of rest is essential for maintaining balance and clarity during life's constant motion.

**Roots Beneath the Waves**:

In this concept, the anchor symbolizes a connection to unseen strength, akin to the roots of a tree that holds firm beneath the surface. Just as the roots of a tree provide stability and support, the anchor represents a source of inner strength that keeps one grounded in times of uncertainty or turmoil. Linking the anchor to hidden roots acknowledges the importance of inner resilience and determination, even when facing overwhelming challenges. This metaphor encourages us to draw strength from within, much like the unseen roots that provide stability to a towering tree.

Anchors serve as powerful metaphors in our lives, providing us with stability and strength in times of uncertainty. Just like how anchors keep boats grounded amidst turbulent waters, they symbolize our ability to stay rooted and resilient when faced with challenges. Whether it's through personal relationships, career choices, or moral values, anchors remind us of the importance of staying true to ourselves and our beliefs. Anchors are not just physical objects, but profound symbols of perseverance and inner strength that guide us through the ebb and flow of life's journey.

God bless you on your journey today.

# 7

# The Anchor Holds!

IN THE BUSTLING PORT town of Booth Bay, there lived an old sea captain named Peter. He was a man of few words but possessed a heart full of faith and wisdom. For years, he had navigated treacherous waters, guided by the light of his steadfast belief. One evening, as a storm brewed on the horizon, Peter prepared to set sail on his ship, the "Knight Commander." He knew the voyage ahead would be perilous, but he trusted in the strength of his faith to guide him through.

Among his crew was a young sailor named Lemuel, eager and full of questions. Lemuel approached Captain Peter, his eyes filled with uncertainty. "Captain," he said, "how do you remain so calm in the face of such a fierce storm?"

As the waves crashed against the hull of the Night Commander, Captain Peter turned to Lemuel with a reassuring smile. He recounted tales of past journeys, each one a testament to his unshakable faith. Through his stories, Captain Peter imparted not only knowledge of the sea but also the importance of trust and belief in the face of adversity.

The crew of the Knight Commander listened intently, their hearts uplifted by the captain's words. During the storm, Lemuel learned from Captain Peter that true strength includes faith, besides skill and experience. This brought him comfort. And so, guided by the light of their captain's enduring belief, the Knight Commander sailed on through the tempest, a symbol of resilience and hope in the face of uncertainty.

Captain Peter smiled gently and placed a reassuring hand on Lemuel's shoulder. "Lemuel," he began. "We have equipped our ship with a strong anchor. When the waters rage, we cast our anchor to keep us steady. In life, faith is our anchor. It holds us firm amidst the storms of doubt and fear."

Captain Peter's words strengthened the Knight Commander's crew. Faith, they learned, wasn't just an idea; it was a powerful guide through hardship. As they continued their journey through the storm, their belief in each other and in a higher power kept their spirits high and their resolve unshaken. The Knight Commander became a beacon of hope in the darkness, a testament to the power of faith and resilience in the face of adversity.

As the storm intensified, the crew of the Knight Commander worked tirelessly to secure the ship against the raging elements. The wind howled, and towering waves crashed against the sturdy vessel, testing the resolve of all on board. However, Captain Peter's unswerving determination and steadfast leadership kept the crew focused and united in the face of adversity.

Standing resolutely at the helm, Captain Peter fixed his gaze on the distant horizon, where he believed a brighter dawn awaited them. Throughout the tumultuous night, Lemuel, a young crew member, watched in awe as the captain guided their ship with a sense of enduring faith and confidence. Despite the chaos and danger surrounding them, Captain Peter's trust in the anchor of faith never faltered.

When the storm finally subsided, leaving the exhausted crew safe but relieved, they marveled at the strength of their ship and the wisdom of their captain. Lemuel, his heart full of respect for Captain Peter and their voyage, approached the captain again. His understanding of the journey on the Knight Commander had deepened.

In a conversation aboard the Knight Commander, Lemuel expressed to Captain Peter the profound realization of how faith serves as an anchor in uncertain times. The captain, with a sense of pride, acknowledged the importance of this lesson and advised Lemuel to always rely on his faith to navigate through life's storms. This wisdom became a guiding principle for the crew of the Knight Commander as they continued their journeys with abiding faith as their anchor.

Captain Peter's words resonated with generations of sailors who found solace because faith could provide strength and stability amidst turbulent waters. The Knight Commander and Captain Peter's teachings offered a beacon of hope during challenging times. Faith, they reminded everyone, remains steadfast despite adversity. Through their shared experiences and abiding belief, the crew of the Knight Commander exemplified the power of faith to weather any tempest that came their way.

In the journey of life, we all encounter challenges and obstacles that can leave us feeling lost and uncertain. During these times, we need a beacon of light to guide us and an anchor for our soul to keep us grounded. These metaphors symbolize the need for hope, guidance, and stability in our lives.

A beacon of light represents a source of hope and guidance. Just as a lighthouse shines its light to help ships navigate through rough waters, a beacon of light in our lives provides us with direction and clarity. It serves as a source of inspiration and motivation, illuminating our path and helping us find our way in times of darkness.

An anchor for the soul represents stability and strength. Just as an anchor keeps a ship steady amidst the tumultuous waves, an anchor for our soul provides us with a sense of security and grounding. It reminds us of our values, beliefs, and purpose, keeping us rooted even when the storms of life threaten to overwhelm us.

Life's uncertainties require guidance; a steady soul needs an anchor. We all need both. These symbols remind us to stay hopeful, resilient, and true to ourselves, no matter what life may throw our way.

Scriptures lead us to seek Christ first, and all else will fall into place. In times of trouble or uncertainty, turning to the teachings and guidance found in the scriptures can provide comfort, direction, and strength. By prioritizing Christ in our lives and following the principles outlined in the scriptures, we can find peace, purpose, and fulfillment. Through prayer, study, and reflection on the scriptures, we can deepen our relationship with Christ and experience His love and grace in our lives. Let us remember to seek Christ first in all things and trust that He will guide us on the path to true happiness and salvation.

God bless you on your journey today.

—◈◆◈—

# 8

# Don't Mess with the Mockingbirds!

G ROWING UP, MY DAD would always caution me about the dangers of disturbing a mockingbird nest while playing in the woods. He emphasized these birds are highly protective of their nests and would not hesitate to attack if they felt threatened. This warning instilled in me a sense of respect for nature and the importance of coexisting with wildlife peacefully.

Mockingbirds, known for their remarkable ability to mimic sounds, are territorial creatures, especially during the nesting season. When a mockingbird pair builds a nest in the woods, they become fiercely protective of their territory. The parent birds perceive any intruder near their nest as a potential threat to their eggs or hatchlings, triggering a defensive response.

My dad's advice was clear: avoid getting too close to a mockingbird nest to prevent any confrontation with the parent birds. Their attacks are not only a means of defense, but also a way of ensuring the survival of their offspring. Understanding and respecting this behavior is crucial for maintaining a harmonious relationship with wildlife in their natural habitat.

The lessons my dad imparted about respecting mockingbird nests in the woods have stayed with me throughout my life. Respecting these birds' nests helps protect their species and allows us to appreciate nature.

I recall one day while observing a mockingbird nest how the parents kept buzzing my head to protect their chicks. I thought it was amusing, but they were serious. One hit the top of my head and sent me running home to safety, followed by the parent birds all the way home.

This is a beautiful and powerful illustration. The image of the mockingbird nest and the protective parents is a vivid reminder of the delicate balance in nature and the unseen forces at work in our lives.

Drawing parallels between the vigilance of birds and the concept of divine guidance can offer profound insights into the mysteries of life. Just as parent birds warn and protect their nests, one can see God's presence as a guiding force that seeks to safeguard and direct us through various means. This analogy invites us to contemplate the subtle ways in which nature reflects deeper spiritual truths.

The vigilant behavior of birds, such as warning signals and protective actions, mirrors the idea of God's constant care and guidance in our lives. Just as the birds communicate through their actions, God may guide us through intuitive whispers or through challenges that push us towards growth and realization. These moments of protection and direction serve as reminders of a higher power watching over us, guiding us towards our true paths.

In contemplating the relationship between the vigilance of birds and divine guidance, we can uncover valuable spiritual lessons. By recognizing the subtle signs and nudges in our lives, we can cultivate a deeper connection to the guiding force of the universe. Just as the birds protect their nests, may we also trust in the unseen hand that guides us towards safety, growth, and fulfillment.

In the story, the concept of an anchor symbolizes stability, hope, and steadfastness in faith. It represents God's unshakable presence as a foundation amid life's storms. Just as an anchor holds a ship steady amid winds and waves, God's guidance can keep us grounded and secure through any challenges we may encounter. The imagery of an anchor serves as a powerful metaphor for the steadfast support and protection that God provides to those who place their trust in Him.

The mockingbird nest serves as a metaphorical anchor for the birds, symbolizing a haven that embodies their home and purpose. Just as the parents' protective instincts act as an anchor, keeping them rooted to their responsibility and steadfast care for their young despite any surrounding dangers. This symbol reminds us of the importance of clinging to our own anchors in faith, trusting in God's provision, and remaining vigilant in our spiritual journey. Just as the mockingbirds find strength and purpose in their nest, we too can find solace and guidance by staying grounded in our beliefs and values.

To stay grounded in our beliefs and values, regular reflection and reaffirmation are important. We can do this through practices such as journaling, meditation, or discussions with trusted individuals who share similar values. It is also beneficial to seek current information and perspectives to ensure that our beliefs are well-informed and adaptable. Actively living out our values through our actions and decisions can help solidify them in our minds and hearts. Overall, staying grounded in our beliefs and values requires ongoing effort, self-awareness, and a commitment to personal growth.

Matthew 5:16 supports this idea: "Let your light so shine before men, that they may see your good works, and glorify your Father which is in heaven." It encourages individuals to highlight their faith through their actions and conduct, bringing glory to God.

Every year, a pair of mockingbirds make their way to our yard, seeking the perfect spot to build their nest. Despite exploring various locations, they always end up returning to the same nest in our grape arbor from the previous year. This choice seems intentional, as the grape leaves provide a natural shield from the sun, keeping the eggs and chicks cool and protected. It is fascinating to witness the meticulous planning and care that the parent birds exhibit, mirroring our own instincts in safeguarding our families.

While observing these mockingbirds, I am careful not to disturb them, but I find joy in watching their activities. As the nesting season progresses, I can sense when the chicks are hatching, as the parent birds display a special behavior. They perch on a nearby limb and engage in a series of vocalizations and movements, displaying their excitement and dedication to their new offspring.

The mockingbirds in our yard highlight nature's beauty and intricacy. They also remind us of the universal drive to nurture and protect.

Mockingbirds exhibit territorial behavior, often selecting a specific yard or area to inhabit and fiercely defending it. This territorial instinct is evident in their behavior as they chase away other birds from the area, sometimes to the discontent of bird enthusiasts. Despite the challenges that come with hosting mockingbirds, their presence adds an element of intrigue and fascination to the bird-watching experience.

In my experience, the mockingbirds in my yard exhibit strong territorial behavior. They are quick to chase away any other birds that come near, asserting their dominance in the area. While this can frustrate, especially for someone who loves birds like me, it is also a testament to the unique nature of these birds.

My bird feeders and birdbaths attract many species, but mockingbirds dominate, preventing others from feeding. Despite the occasional conflicts that arise, I find joy in observing the interactions between the mockingbirds and other birds, appreciating the intricate dynamics of the avian world.

My wife, Renee, often teases me about my bird-feeding habits, claiming that I spend too much money on bird seeds. However, to me, the investment is well worth it. The joy of seeing the diverse array of birds that visit our yard, including the territorial mockingbirds, brings me a sense of fulfillment and connection to the natural world.

In conclusion, the territorial behavior of mockingbirds adds a layer of complexity to the bird-watching experience. While they may be challenging, their presence enriches the ecosystem of our yard and provides endless opportunities for observation and appreciation. Despite the occasional disagreements with my wife over bird seed expenses, I am grateful for the opportunity to witness the beauty and intricacies of these fascinating creatures. They keep me anchored!

# 9

# The Enigmatic Anchor

THE OCEAN STRETCHED ENDLESSLY before Adrian, but beneath its surface, he could sense a profound stillness. It was as though the sea held secrets far older than time. As a sailor, Adrian had always found solace on the water, but tonight, the ocean felt different—almost alive. Ever since his wife's passing, Adrian had carried a void within him, one that no horizon or storm could fill. He had set out alone, searching for answers, though he wasn't sure where—or to whom—to direct his pleas. When his net snagged on something below, Adrian peered overboard, his lantern casting faint light on the waves. He hauled up a massive, rusted anchor, its surface engraved with intricate symbols that seemed to shift as if breathing. A strange energy pulsed from it, not menacing but beckoning. Compelled by a force beyond his understanding,

Adrian reached out and touched the anchor.

In that moment, a wave of sensations washed over Adrian. The touch of the anchor sent shivers down his spine, and a warmth spread through his body. It was as if the anchor held a piece of the universe's mystery, whispering ancient truths to him. Adrian felt a connection forming, a bond between himself and this enigmatic object. As he gazed at the shifting symbols, a sense of purpose stirred within him; he felt this encounter was fated, a turning point in his journey of healing and self-discovery.

With hesitant reverence, Adrian traced the intricate patterns etched on the anchor's surface. Each stroke of his finger unlocked an additional layer of meaning, a deeper understanding of the forces at play. The anchor no longer felt like a mere object, but a gateway to realms beyond comprehension. Adrian closed his eyes, allowing the energy to envelop him and guide him towards a truth he had been seeking without knowing.

As the night wore on, Adrian remained by the side of the anchor, lost in contemplation and wonder. The ocean whispered ancient lullabies; the stars danced in silent admiration, and Adrian felt a sense of peace settling within him. A newfound sense of purpose and belonging replaced the void that had plagued his heart. With the anchor as his silent companion, Adrian knew his journey was far from over. It was just beginning—a voyage into the depths of the unknown, guided by the enigmatic whispers of the sea.

The world dissolved in a cascade of light. When Adrian opened his eyes, he stood on a shore bathed in golden light, where the air hummed with an almost divine presence. A figure appeared, shimmering and indistinct, their voice a melody of calm and wisdom. "You have been called here," the figure said, "not to escape, but to remember."

As Adrian gazed out at the horizon, he felt a sense of anticipation and curiosity stirring within him. What secrets lay hidden in the depths of the ocean? What truths awaited him on this mysterious shore? Wonder filled Adrian's heart as he began this new chapter. He was ready for whatever adventures awaited.

Adrian fell to his knees, overcome with emotion. "Why?" he asked, his voice trembling. "I've lost everything. What remains for me to remember?" The figure extended a glowing hand, and the ocean before them stirred. From its depths rose waves—not of water but of light, each one revealing a unique moment from Adrian's life.

He saw himself as a young boy, laughing with his siblings. He relived the joy of meeting his wife and the love that had defined his life. But then came darker memories—times of anger, loss, and grief. He looked away, unable to bear them. The ocean's memories, both joyful and painful, unfolded before Adrian, offering a glimpse into his past and guiding him towards a new understanding of himself.

"You cannot heal while running from your pain," the figure said. "It is part of the sacred thread that weaves your life together. You are not alone, Adrian. The same force that moves the tides and lights the stars flows through you. It connects all that was, is, and will be." As Adrian watched, the scenes shifted again—this time to moments he had ignored in his grief. Friends who had offered their support, family who had reached out to help, strangers who had shown him kindness. He realized, with a pang of humility, that even in his darkest moments, the world had been calling him back to the light. Tears streamed down his face. "I don't know how to carry this weight," he whispered.

In this profound moment of self-realization, Adrian came to understand the interconnectedness of his pain

with the fabric of his existence. The figure's words resonated deeply within him, urging him to confront his
pain rather than evade it. Shifting scenes confronted Adrian with the overlooked acts of compassion and love surrounding him during his darkest hours. This revelation
brought tears to his eyes as he acknowledged the lifelines
extended to him, waiting for him to grasp them.

As Adrian stood at the precipice of his emotions, he
grappled with the weight of his suffering. The burden
seemed overwhelming, threatening to engulf him in its
darkness. Yet, within that vulnerability, a glimmer of hope
emerged—a realization that by embracing his pain, he
could begin the journey towards healing. With the world's
unseen forces guiding him, Adrian took a tentative step
forward, ready to confront his pain and embark on the
path towards wholeness.

In a moment of despair, Adrian experienced a transformative encounter with a mysterious figure who guided
him to surrender his burdens to a greater current. As he
touched the glowing anchor, a profound sense of peace
washed over him, replacing his grief with an unshakable
connection to something beyond himself.

Awakening on his boat, Adrian found the anchor now

resting in the bow, symbolizing the newfound strength and hope within him. The once turbulent ocean now shimmered with a divine light, reflecting the profound transformation within Adrian. He set sail; his heart full of hope. He embraced the journey not to escape his pain but to live fully and carry the light of his new connection.

# 10

# Divine Encounters that Anchor Our Faith

❧

O N A FATEFUL DAY, Evelyn Smith, aged forty-four, found herself in unfamiliar territory as she entered the hospital because of agony on her right side. Initially diagnosed with appendicitis, she underwent surgery for the removal of her appendix. However, the excruciating pain persisted, prompting her husband, Ben, to rush her back to the hospital through the emergency room the following night. This unexpected turn of events marked the beginning of a medical journey filled with uncertainty and challenges.

Being a woman of faith, Evelyn assured her husband, Ben, that she would be all right. However, after experiencing some concerning symptoms, she sought medical attention. Tests later that night revealed an enormous mass in a very precarious spot underneath her right breast. The news was unexpected and unsettling, but Evelyn remained hopeful and determined to face this health challenge with courage and faith. She and Ben prayed on the side of her hospital bed that God would direct them in which way to go. Her doctor scheduled Evelyn for a biopsy the following morning.

The following day, the doctors in the operating room found that the enormous mass had metastasized to her breast bones and was dangerously close to her heart. It was cancer, and the most aggressive kind!

Dr. White devastated Evelyn and Ben with the news. What would they tell her two precious children? How would they explain it to them?

Doctors scheduled Evelyn for radiation the following morning, planning an aggressive approach to address a mass in her body. That evening, filled with hope and faith, Evelyn and her husband Ben prayed fervently for a miraculous intervention. A miraculous answer to their prayers defied medical explanation—two days later, the doctors could not find the concerning mass. The disappearance of the cancer left the medical team astounded.

Subsequent tests confirmed the astonishing news: Evelyn was completely free of cancer. Doctors discharged her to go home the next day, scheduling a follow-up scan in a week. To everyone's relief and joy, the scan came back negative, affirming the miraculous healing that had taken place. Evelyn's journey was a testament to the power of faith, hope, and the unexplainable wonders that can occur in the face of adversity.

The anchor doesn't just stop us from drifting—it roots us, giving us security and hope even when the seas grow rough. These divine encounters can show how people cling to such spiritual anchors as a source of strength, faith, and inspiration. In times of uncertainty and turbulence, these spiritual anchors provide a sense of stability and guidance that helps individuals navigate through life's challenges with resilience and courage.

Spiritual anchors come in various forms, such as religious beliefs, practices, and communities. For many, their faith serves as an unshakable foundation that provides comfort and reassurance in times of need. Through prayer, meditation, and connection with a higher power, individuals can find peace and solace amidst the chaos of the world. The support of a spiritual community can offer a sense of belonging and unity, strengthening one's resolve and commitment to their beliefs.

Spiritual anchors can also serve as sources of inspiration and motivation. By aligning their actions with their spiritual values, individuals can lead purpose-driven lives that are guided by principles of compassion, integrity, and love. This sense of moral grounding not only benefits the individual but also has a ripple effect on the community, fostering a culture of kindness and understanding.

We cannot underestimate the power of spiritual anchors. They provide individuals with a sense of security, hope, and purpose that transcends the challenges of everyday life. By cultivating a strong connection to their spiritual beliefs and practices, individuals can weather any storm and emerge stronger and more resilient. Spiritual anchors serve as guiding lights that illuminate the path towards inner peace and fulfillment.

Amid his grief, a father sought solace within the walls of the cathedral. As he kneeled in prayer, the sunlight streaming through the vibrant stained glass caught his eye, illuminating his tear-streaked face. In that moment, it felt as though the hand of God was reaching out to him, offering a glimmer of hope amidst the darkness of his loss. The cathedral's peaceful atmosphere calmed him. He found strength and guidance in God's presence, a constant even during troubled times. It served as a reminder that, like the sturdy anchor of a ship in a stormy sea, God was there to steady him and provide comfort in his time of need.

Prayer can serve as a powerful anchor in one's life, providing a sense of peace and grounding that helps navigate through the uncertainties and challenges of life. For many individuals, prayer is not just a routine practice but a profound source of strength and resilience.

When a woman experiences a deep sense of peace during prayer, it can feel like being enveloped in a comforting embrace. This feeling of peace becomes her anchor, grounding her in moments of uncertainty and doubt. It serves as a reminder of hope and the divine, empowering her to face life's challenges with grace and resilience.

In times of turmoil and confusion, the practice of prayer can be a guiding light, offering solace and strength to those who seek it. By cultivating a deep connection through prayer, individuals can find the anchor they need to weather life's storms with courage and faith.

Standing by the ocean, a man senses God's presence in the crashing waves and steady horizon. The ocean, vast and constant, becomes his anchor, symbolizing God's steadfast stability amidst life's chaos. The rhythmic sound of the waves reminds us of God's eternal love and the enduring strength found in nature. As the man gazes out at the expanse of the ocean, he finds solace in the beauty and power of nature, feeling a deep connection to something greater than himself. In this moment of reflection, he can find peace and clarity, grounded by the immense presence of the ocean and the divine energy it represents.

And so, the anchor becomes not just a relic of the past but a living symbol—a steadying force amidst the unpredictable tides of life. Whether through miraculous events or moments of profound peace, it reminds us that no matter how fierce the storm, we are never adrift. Faith, like an anchor, grips us, offering hope, purpose, and the assurance that something greater than ourselves tethers us.

God bless you on your journey today.

# 11

# Anchored in God's Parables

T HERE ARE MANY PARABLES in both the Bible and
in life that deal with being anchored in God's
Word. I will list just a few here to give us bearing. Dr.
Samuel Greenwood always said that a parable is "an earthly
story with a heavenly meaning."

Parable 1: **The Modern Samaritan**:

- Biblical Reference: The Parable of the Good
  Samaritan (Luke 10:25-37)

- Key Lesson: Love your neighbor and show compassion to those in need, regardless of their back-
  ground or circumstances.

In the heart of a bustling city, where time is always of
the essence, a well-dressed businesswoman rushes to an
important meeting. As she hurriedly navigates the crowd-

ed streets, her mind consumed with deadlines and obligations, a sudden commotion catches her attention. An elderly man has collapsed on the sidewalk, surrounded by indifferent passersby lost in the rhythm of urban life.

Amidst the apathy, a ray of light emerges as a compassionate nurse. Despite being already late for her shift, she pauses without hesitation and rushes to the aid of the fallen man. Ignoring the disapproving glances and the ticking clock, she tends to him with care and urgency, ensuring that he receives the medical attention he desperately needs. With unwavering dedication, she stays by his side until he is safe in the hands of professionals.

This poignant encounter serves as a modern-day rendition of the timeless Parable of the Good Samaritan, a tale that transcends generations and underscores the essence of humanity. It reminds us of the inherent goodness that lies within each of us and the profound impact of extending a helping hand, even when it comes at a personal cost. Selfless acts, rare in our self-centered world, highlight the daily importance of compassion and empathy.

The themes of compassion, mercy, and neighborly love are part of this story.

Parable 2: **The Lost Wallet**:

- Biblical Reference: The Parable of the Lost Coin (Luke 15:8–10)

- Key Lesson: Seek and value what you have lost and find joy in discovering it.

In a bustling metropolis, a young man came across a wallet filled with a substantial amount of cash lying on the sidewalk. He felt tempted by the thought of using the money to pay his overdue rent and bills. Despite the financial strain he was under, the young man made a decision that would change his life. Instead of keeping the money for himself, he embarked on a mission to find the rightful owner of the wallet.

After some diligent detective work, the young man successfully located the owner of the wallet, an elderly woman who had tearfully reported it missing, along with her life savings. The young man's return of the wallet, complete with all the money, shocked and elated the woman. Gratitude overflowed from her heart as she thanked him profusely for his honesty and kindness.

Over time, a beautiful friendship blossomed between the young man and the elderly woman. They shared stories, laughter, and wisdom, finding a deep connection that transcended the initial act of returning the lost wallet. Their bond became a testament to the power of integrity and doing what is right in a world often clouded by self-interest and greed.

This parable mirrors the timeless lesson of the Parable of the Lost Coin, illustrating the profound impact of choosing honesty and compassion over personal gain. It serves as a reminder that true wealth lies not in material possessions but in the richness of human relationships and the integrity of one's character.

The themes of integrity, redemption, restoration, trust, and friendship should lift our spirits in this story.

Parable 3: **The Startup Seeds**:

- Biblical Reference: The Parable of the Sower (Matthew 13:1-23, Mark 4:1-20, Luke 8:4-15)

- Key Lesson: The different responses to the word of God and the importance of cultivating a receptive and fruitful heart.

In a tale reminiscent of the Parable of the Sower, a group of friends embarks on a journey to start a business together. Among them, one friend stands out for their excessive ambition, leading to reckless spending that causes the business to fail.

Another friend, on the opposite end of the spectrum, embodies extreme caution, often missing crucial opportunities for growth and development. However, it is the third friend who balances risk and caution, demonstrating wisdom, patience, and perseverance in their approach to business decisions. Through their steadfast efforts, this friend successfully navigates the challenges of entrepreneurship, flourishing the business.

This parable serves as a poignant reminder of the importance of prudence and balance in pursuit of success. Just as the seeds sown in the Parable of the Sower require nurturing and care to flourish, so, too, does a business venture demand thoughtful consideration and strategic planning. By embodying the virtues of wisdom, patience, and perseverance, individuals can overcome obstacles and setbacks, paving the way for sustainable growth and prosperity in their entrepreneurial endeavors.

The themes of wisdom and discernment, perseverance, and fruitfulness highlight this parable.

Parable 4: **The Grateful Customer**:

- Biblical Reference: The Parable of the Talents (Matthew 25:14-30)

- Key Lesson: The importance of using the resources and opportunities given to us wisely and generously, and the rewards of faithfulness.

In a small town, there was a struggling cafe owner who faced financial challenges in her business. Despite her own hardships, she always helped her customers. One day, a loyal customer forgot his wallet and couldn't pay for his meal. Instead of turning him away, the cafe owner generously offered him a free meal, showing kindness and compassion in a time of need.

Grateful for her generosity, the customer returned to the cafe and brought along many friends to dine there. These new patrons enjoyed the food and atmosphere so much that they became regular customers, bringing in much-needed revenue to the struggling cafe. The loyalty of these new customers saved the cafe from closing, and the business thrived once again.

This heartwarming story reflects the timeless lesson of the Parable of the Talents, emphasizing the importance of generosity, trust, and kindness, even in the face of uncertainty. The cafe owner's kindness to one customer saved her business. In the same way, small, insignificant gestures of faith and generosity can lead to unexpected success and blessings.

The themes of generosity, faithfulness, and the impact of minor acts are keys to this fruitful parable.

Each of these modern parables can offer relatable insights and moral lessons that are deeply anchored in biblical truths. I hope these resonate with you!

——❖——

# 12

# Illuminating Anchors

I AM CRAFTING THIS tome with the theme of anchors, illuminating their profound significance in the tapestry of our lives. In this article, I would like to present the following biblical scriptures for your reflection:

- Psalm 23

- Romans 5:8

- Mark 3:34-36

- Matthew 4

- Hebrews 6:19

Psalm 23 stands as perhaps the most beloved scripture in the sacred tapestry of the Bible. In the Psalm, King David describes his life as being deeply anchored in God. In

Psalm 23, he eloquently portrays the Lord as his shepherd, providing comfort and guidance through every valley and over every hill. This profound relationship with the divine acts as an anchor, grounding him in times of uncertainty and fear.

The imagery of green pastures and still waters symbolize peace and renewal, illustrating how David's trust in God brings tranquility and rejuvenation to his soul. The metaphor of the shepherd highlights a sense of protection and care, reinforcing the idea that even when walking through the darkest valleys, he is never alone.

Just as an anchor secures a ship, preventing it from drifting away with the tides, David's faith anchors his spirit, granting him the courage to face challenges with confidence and hope. The scriptures deeply resonate with this theme; Romans 5:8 affirms the depth of God's love, and Hebrews 6:19 describes hope as "a sure and steadfast anchor of the soul."

These passages collectively remind us that anchoring our lives in faith offers us resilience, guiding us through the ebbs and flows of existence with grace and assurance.

Romans 5:8 states, "But God shows his own love for us in this: While we were still sinners, Christ died for us." This profound verse underscores the unconditional and sacrificial nature of divine love, which serves as a foundational anchor for believers. It emphasizes that the love of God is not contingent upon our perfection or worthiness but is a steadfast force that grounds us, offering redemption and hope in the face of our imperfections. This unwavering love acts as an anchor, providing strength and stability and encouraging us to embrace grace and move forward with renewed purpose and confidence.

Mark 3:34–36, a passage that invites us to reflect on the concept of spiritual kinship, presents a moment where Jesus redefines the notion of family. He looks around at those seated in a circle around him and says, "Here are my mother and my brothers! Whoever does God's will is my brother, sister, and mother." This declaration emphasizes that genuine connection and belonging are not solely determined by blood, but by shared faith and purpose.

In the context of anchors, this teaching highlights the importance of community as a stabilizing force in our spiritual journey. Just as an anchor holds a ship steady, our relationships with those who share our values and beliefs can provide support and strength. The bond of spiritual family creates a network of encouragement and solidarity, helping us remain grounded in our convictions even amidst life's challenges.

This sense of belonging within a community of faith serves as an anchor, reinforcing our identity and purpose. It reminds us we are part of something larger than ourselves, connected by our collective commitment to living out God's will. As we navigate the complexities of life, these relationships offer us a sense of stability and assurance, much like the comforting presence of an anchor in a stormy sea.

In this way, Mark 3:34–36 complements the overarching theme of anchors, demonstrating how our faith and relationships can work together to provide a foundation of strength and resilience in our lives.

Matthew 4: The Temptation of Jesus presents a profound narrative that explores the theme of spiritual anchoring through the trials faced by Jesus in the wilderness. After fasting forty days and forty nights, the tempter confronted Jesus with three significant challenges. Each temptation targets a fundamental aspect of human desire: hunger, power, and identity.

The first temptation urged Jesus to turn stones into bread, appealing to his physical hunger. However, Jesus responds with scripture, asserting that "Man shall not live on bread alone, but on every word that comes from the mouth of God." This response highlights the importance of spiritual sustenance and reliance on divine wisdom as a foundational anchor.

The second temptation involves the tempter taking Jesus to the pinnacle of the temple, daring him to throw himself down to be saved by angels, thus proving his divine sonship. Jesus counters by emphasizing trust in God without seeking to test Him, reinforcing faith as an anchor that does not require constant validation.

Finally, the tempter offers Jesus all the kingdoms of the world in exchange for worship. Jesus' refusal, grounded in his devotion to worship God alone, underscores the significance of unwavering allegiance to divine values over worldly gains.

Throughout these trials, Jesus remains firmly anchored in his identity and mission, rooted in his relationship with God. This passage serves as a powerful illustration of how anchoring oneself in faith and scripture can provide the steadfastness needed to overcome life's challenges. It reminds us that our spiritual anchor is not only a source of strength but also a guide that directs us toward our true purpose and calling.

Hebrews 6:19 beautifully encapsulates the essence of hope as "a sure and steadfast anchor of the soul, a hope that enters the inner place behind the veil." This scripture paints a vivid picture of hope as a secure anchor, grounding us amidst life's uncertainties and connecting us to the divine. It draws on the imagery of an anchor to emphasize stability and assurance, reminding us that our hope is not fleeting or superficial, but deeply rooted in a promise that transcends the temporal.

This verse invites us to envision hope as a powerful force that holds us steady, much like an anchor holds a ship in place during turbulent seas. It assures us that no matter how fierce the storms of life may be, we have an anchor that is firm and reliable, anchored in the very presence of God.

The reference to "the inner place behind the curtain" alludes to the Holy of Holies in the temple, a sacred space symbolizing the presence of God. This imagery suggests that our hope is not just an abstract concept but a tangible connection to the divine, offering us access to grace and strength beyond what we can see or understand.

In life's voyage, where we encounter both calm and tempest, Hebrews 6:19 reassures us that our hope in God's promises provides an unshakeable foundation. It encourages us to hold fast to this hope, allowing it to guide us through life's challenges with courage and faith. Anchoring our souls in this hope empowers us to face each day confidently, knowing that a love that is eternal and unchanging securely holds us.

# 13

# Mama - My Anchor

GROWING UP IN HELENA, Georgia, my mama held
the family together as the anchor. She was a woman
of strength and dependability, always striving for perfection in everything she did. Her words carried weight, and
we, her children, knew better than to disobey her. The
consequences of going against her wishes were severe, and
we quickly learned to heed her guidance. Mama's presence
in our lives was the rock that kept us grounded and taught
us the importance of respect and obedience.

Every morning and afternoon, rain or shine, my mother
walked a mile with us to and from school. With my dad
using the only car for work, walking became our daily routine. Despite her own busy schedule, Mama worked tirelessly to support our family. By day, she was a cook in the
school lunchroom, and by night, she worked at a restau-

rant until midnight. On Saturdays, she took on the chores of washing clothes and cleaning the house. Through her unwavering dedication and hard work, Mama became the anchor of our family. Her love and sacrifices never went unnoticed, and we were grateful for everything she did for us.

Mama's story is a testament to the power of love, hard work, and unwavering dedication. Through every challenge and triumph, she remained a beacon of hope and inspiration for her children, leaving an indelible mark on our hearts and lives.

A mother, as the anchor of a family, embodies strength, love, and resilience. Her role extends far beyond daily tasks; she is the emotional and spiritual center, providing unwavering support and stability.

A Mother's Day often begins before the sun rises and ends long after it sets. She prepares meals, organizes schedules, and ensures that everyone has what they need. But her contributions go deeper than the physical. She is a source of comfort, a healer of wounds, both physical and emotional, and a guide through life's many challenges.

In times of crisis, the family looks to her for reassurance. Her calm presence and steady hands navigated the storm, turning chaos into order. She listens without judgment, offering advice and wisdom drawn from her own experiences. Her words can soothe fears and inspire confidence, reminding her children that they are never alone.

A mother's love is unconditional, embracing her children as they are, while encouraging them to grow into their best selves. She celebrates their successes and stands by them through failures, teaching them that both are valuable parts of the journey. Her sacrifices, though often unseen, form the foundation upon which her family builds its dreams.

Her life is a delicate balance of selflessness and self-care. She nurtures her own passions and interests, knowing that her well-being is crucial to her family's happiness. She finds strength in her community, drawing on the support of friends and loved ones and sharing her own wisdom in return.

The life of a mother as an anchor is one of profound love and dedication. Her unwavering presence and boundless heart weave her legacy into the fabric of her family's lives, powerfully showing her strength.

Mama was quite the seamstress, always taking in clothing to work on in our home for small pittances in return, but every dime helped the family. Her sacrifices were countless and unrepayable. Mama always said that all she wanted at her passing was a single rose on her casket. She was simple, yet complicated.

Mama's skill with a needle and thread was unmatched, and her dedication to providing for her family through her sewing talents was unwavering. In every stitch, there was love woven into the fabric, a testament to her selflessness and devotion to those she held dear.

Her humble request for a single rose at her funeral speaks volumes about the modesty and grace with which she lived her life. Mama found beauty in simplicity and cherished the insignificant gestures that held deep meaning.

Mama's life profoundly affected our family and countless others through her kindness and craftsmanship. Though she may be gone, her legacy lives on in the memories we hold dear and the values she instilled in us.

Mama was indeed simple, yet complicated in the most beautiful of ways. Her strength, resilience, and unwavering love continue to inspire us each day.

Mothers always stand out in both art and literature. Here are a few of them.

In literature, here are a few examples of dedicated mothers.

1. **Marmee (Mrs. March)** from *Little Women*

Louisa May Alcott's novel "Little Women" features Marmee, also known as Mrs. March, as a central character. Despite the family's financial struggles and the absence of her husband, who is serving in the Civil War, Marmee remains a pillar of strength and support for her family. Her unwavering love, kindness, and resilience define her character in the face of adversity. In the novel, Marmee teaches her daughter's valuable life lessons about compassion, selflessness, and love. Her guidance and wisdom play a significant role in shaping the moral development of her daughters and are instrumental in helping them navigate the challenges of growing up in a changing world. Marmee's character serves as an inspirational example of maternal strength and unconditional love.

1. **Molly Weasley** from Harry Potter series by J.K. Rowling

Molly Weasley is the matriarch of the Weasley family in J. K. Rowling's series. She fiercely dedicates herself to her children and provides a warm and loving home for her family. Molly goes beyond to protect and care for her loved ones, highlighting her strong maternal instincts. She extends her motherly care not only to her own children but also to Harry Potter, treating him as one of her own. Molly's character exemplifies strength, compassion, and unwavering love in the face of adversity.

1. **Ma Joad** in *The Grapes of Wrath* by John Steinbeck

Ma Joad is the anchor of the Joad family in John Steinbeck's novel, The Grapes of Wrath. Throughout the story, she serves as a guiding force, leading her family through the challenges of the Great Depression. Ma Joad's strength, determination, and unwavering love for her family make her a powerful symbol of maternal dedication. Despite the hardships they face, Ma Joad remains a source of stability and support for her loved ones, highlighting her resilience and unwavering spirit in the face of adversity. Steinbeck portrays Ma Joad as a beacon of hope and strength, embodying the enduring power of a mother's love.

In art, we learn of the following examples:

1. **"Whistler's Mother"** by James McNeill Whistler

"Whistler's Mother," formally titled "Arrangement in Gray and Black No. 1," is an iconic painting by the artist James McNeill Whistler. The artwork portrays the artist's mother in a serene and contemplative pose, capturing a moment of quiet reflection and maternal presence. This painting has become a symbol of maternal strength and devotion, resonating with audiences around the world. Whistler's careful composition and use of color in "Whistler's Mother" create a sense of timeless elegance and emotional depth, making it a significant piece in art history.

## 1. The Madonna and Child

Throughout art history, the depiction of the Madonna and Child has been a central theme in Christian art. These paintings and sculptures celebrate the bond between the Virgin Mary and Jesus, highlighting the mother's love and dedication.

These examples highlight the enduring power and influence of dedicated mothers in both literature and art. Their stories and depictions continue to inspire and resonate with audiences across generations.

Everyone needs an anchor. Mama was mine!

# 14

# Ole Henry - Anchor of the Forest

⧓

O LE HENRY STOOD AMID the large, wooded forest of pine trees in South Georgia. The forest stretched as far as the eye could see. The fresh scent of resin was rich and inviting. Ole Henry, surviving most other trees, had existed for generations, and stood taller and prouder than the rest. He had witnessed the passage of time and the changing of the seasons for over a century.

Ole Henry, with his thick trunk and sprawling branches, served as a symbol of resilience and endurance in the forest. Countless storms and harsh winters weathered and gnarled the bark of his trunk, leaving their scars. His roots delved deep into the earth, anchoring him firmly in place as he withstood the test of time.

Throughout his long life, Ole Henry had provided shelter and sustenance to countless creatures of the forest. Birds nested in his branches, squirrels scurried up and down his trunk, and insects made their homes in the crevices of his bark. He had seen generations of wildlife come and go, each finding solace and protection in his sturdy presence.

As the seasons changed, Ole Henry transformed with them. Fresh green needles adorned his branches in the spring, shimmering in the sunlight. In the summer, he provided a cool respite from the heat with his dense canopy of foliage. In the fall, his needles turned a brilliant shade of gold, painting the forest with hues of amber and ochre. And in the winter, he stood stark and bare, his branches dusted with a layer of frost and snow.

Ole Henry's presence in the forest was a reminder of the enduring power of nature and the importance of preserving its beauty and diversity. As he stood tall and proud amidst the whispering pines, he was a living testament to the strength and majesty of the natural world.

Ole Henry, a towering pine tree, stood as a silent witness to the passage of time in the vast forest. He'd witnessed many things during his lifetime: devastating wildfires, joyful family picnics, and lumberjacks felling his companions.

Yet, miraculously, Ole Henry remained untouched, a symbol of resilience and endurance in the face of man's relentless pursuit of timber. The lumberjacks, in awe of his majestic presence and venerable age, always spared him, acknowledging his role as a living monument to the forest's history. Ole Henry's story became a legend among the trees, a testament to the power of nature and the enduring spirit of life in the wilderness.

One crisp morning, the roar of chainsaws shattered the stillness of the forest. A team of lumberjacks had arrived, their mission clear: to perform a clear cut, felling every tree in the designated area for the mill. Ole Henry, an ancient pine tree standing tall and proud amidst the younger pines, felt a pang of sadness as the sounds of destruction echoed through the woods. The younger trees trembled with fear, knowing that their time might soon end.

As the lumberjacks approached Ole Henry, their chainsaws revving with a deafening noise, the old tree braced himself for what was to come. He had stood in that forest for over a century, witnessing the changing seasons and sheltering countless birds and small animals within his branches. Now, faced with the inevitability of his own demise, he could only hope that his sacrifice would not be in vain.

The first cut of the chainsaw sent vibrations through Ole Henry's trunk, a sensation he had never experienced before. The old pine tree closed his eyes, whispering a silent goodbye as the lumberjacks worked to fell him. He had lived in the forest for many years. And as he fell, crashing to the forest floor with a thunderous roar, Ole Henry knew his legacy would live on in the memories of those who had known him.

As Ole Henry stood atop the towering pine trees, he couldn't help but ponder the rich history of his kind. For centuries, people have highly valued pine trees for their versatile properties. The wood, tar, and resin extracted from pine trees have played a crucial role in various industries, particularly in shipbuilding.

In the early days of maritime exploration, pine tar and resin were indispensable materials used for waterproofing and preserving wooden ships. The natural properties of pine tar made it an excellent sealant, protecting the vessels from the harsh elements of the sea. Shipbuilders used the pine tree resin for its adhesive qualities, securing the hulls and preventing leaks.

People often sought the tall and majestic pines, renowned for their straight trunks and sturdy branches, for their suitability as masts and spars. These essential components of a ship's rigging provided structural support and stability, guiding sailors on their perilous voyages across the vast oceans.

As Ole Henry's thoughts drifted amidst the rustling pine needles, he marveled at the enduring legacy of his kind in shaping the maritime history of seafaring nations. The pine tree, with its resilience and adaptability, had left an indelible mark on the evolution of shipbuilding practices, symbolizing the enduring bond between nature and human ingenuity.

Ole Henry, a seasoned pine, passionately believed in the importance of clear-cutting as a fundamental practice in forestry management. He understood that selective tree removal would encourage fresh growth and maintain the forest's overall health. Despite the initial visual impact of clear-cutting, Ole Henry found solace knowing that his sacrifice would pave the way for the next generation of pines to thrive. He recognized the cyclical nature of forestry, where his sacrifices today would ensure the sustainability of the forest for future generations. Ole Henry's dedication to responsible forest management exemplifies the balance between human intervention and natural processes in maintaining healthy and vibrant ecosystems.

With a final deep breath, Ole Henry stood tall and proud amidst the towering trees of the forest. The chainsaw's blade bit into his trunk, and he fell, the echoes of nature's protest ringing in his ears. As he tumbled to the ground, he whispered a silent prayer for the future of the forest and the new life that would soon take root in his place.

In the following months, the once lush and vibrant forest underwent a transformation. The cleared area now bore the scars of human intervention, with the stumps of the fallen trees standing as silent sentinels, solemn reminders of the forest that once thrived there. The landscape appeared barren, stripped of its former glory.

However, amidst the desolation, signs of hope emerged. Tiny saplings, tender and green, pushed their way through the scorched earth, their roots seeking nourishment and their leaves reaching for the sky with newfound determination. These young trees symbolized the resilience and tenacity of nature, a testament to the cycle of renewal that governed the forest's existence.

As time passed, the once barren land flourished once again. The saplings grew taller, their branches intertwining to create a new canopy, while wildflowers and shrubs carpeted the forest floor. The forest was reborn, a testament to the enduring power of nature to heal and regenerate in the face of adversity.

And so Ole Henry's sacrifice was not in vain. His fall had paved the way for new life to take root, ensuring that the forest would continue to thrive and flourish for generations to come. Renewal is a cycle. Death gives way to life; destruction leads to regeneration. All this highlights nature's interconnectedness.

The legacy of the pines lived on, their story etched into the annals of history. As the young trees grew, they carried with them the wisdom and strength of their ancestors, ready to face the challenges of the future.

The towering pines had weathered countless storms, their roots delving deep into the earth for nourishment and stability. Each tree stood tall, anchored in their testament to resilience and endurance. Through the changing seasons and shifting landscapes, the pines remained steadfast, providing shelter and solace to creatures big and small. Their branches whispered ancient tales to the wind, weaving a tapestry of memories that spanned generations. The legacy of the pines was not just a story of the past but a living, breathing connection to the land and all who called it home.

# 15

# Anchored in His Presence

J AMES FOUND HIMSELF ONE day amid a full-blown
life crisis. While struggling with self-doubt and overwhelming challenges, James feels like he's drowning in a
sea of problems. One evening, while James was reading his
Bible, he came across the story of Jesus walking on water in
Matthew 14:22–33. Inspired by the passage, James learns
the importance of keeping his eyes fixed on Jesus, even
when the storms of life seem insurmountable.

As James delves deeper into the story of Jesus walking on water, he discovers a profound lesson about faith
and perseverance. Like Peter, who sank when he took his
eyes off Jesus, James learned to focus on Jesus amid life's
storms. Through this biblical narrative, James finds renewed strength and courage to confront his own challenges with a resilient spirit.

The metaphor of walking on water becomes a powerful symbol for James as he navigates his own turbulent waters. By anchoring himself in faith and trust, James sees glimmers of hope amidst the darkness of his struggles. The story of Jesus walking on water serves as a guiding light for James, reminding him that with unwavering faith, even the impossible becomes possible.

In the days that follow, James embarks on a journey of self-discovery and spiritual growth. By embracing the teachings of the Bible and drawing strength from his newfound perspective, James weathers the storms of life with a renewed sense of purpose and resilience. Faith transforms James, giving him the courage to face challenges. With God's help, he believes he can overcome anything.

One of the prominent themes that resonates throughout the story is faith in uncertainty. The protagonist, James, undergoes a transformation where he learns to place his trust in God's presence and guidance, particularly when the future appears ambiguous and unpredictable. Despite facing challenges and obstacles, James finds solace in his unwavering belief that God is with him, providing him with the strength and direction needed to navigate through life's uncertainties. Through his journey, James exemplifies the power of faith in overcoming doubts and fears, discovering a sense of peace and purpose amid uncertainty.

In literature, the theme of Divine Intervention is a recurring motif that often symbolizes moments of spiritual awakening or guidance. The story of Peter and Jesus, where Jesus saves Peter from drowning, notably exemplifies this theme of divine intervention and protection.

Similarly, in a modern context, the character James experiences a similar divine intervention that serves to renew his faith and provide him with guidance and support. These instances of divine intervention highlight the belief in a higher power and the idea that supernatural forces can intervene in human lives to bring about positive change or enlightenment.

Literature's exploration of divine intervention prompts reflection on faith, fate, and spirituality's impact on human experience and self-understanding. It also encourages a broader understanding of the world.

"Stepping Out" is a central theme in the narrative of James, who draws inspiration from the biblical story to take courageous steps in both his personal and professional life. These bold actions result in transformative changes and significant personal growth for him. By embracing faith and stepping out of his comfort zone, James navigates challenges and opportunities with resilience and determination. His journey exemplifies the power of bold faith in driving positive outcomes and shaping one's destiny.

In Matthew 14:27, we find a powerful message of courage and reassurance from Jesus to His disciples during a time of fear and uncertainty. The Sea of Galilee provides the setting; there, the disciples battled fierce winds and waves in their boat. Amid this chaos, Jesus appears walking on the water towards them. Understandably, this miraculous sight fills the disciples with fear and confusion.

However, Jesus immediately speaks words of comfort and encouragement to them, saying, "Take courage! It is I! Do not be afraid." This statement not only acknowledges His presence and identity but also serves as a reminder to the disciples that they need not fear the unknown when they have faith in Him. This verse is a powerful reminder for us all that in moments of fear and doubt, we can find strength and courage in the unwavering presence of Jesus.

**Anchoring Our Souls with Jesus**

In the journey of life, it is imperative that we learn to anchor our souls with Jesus. By placing our trust in His power and will, we can find the strength and sustenance needed to navigate through the challenges and uncertainties that come our way. Jesus serves as our beacon of hope and a source of steadfast support, guiding us through the storms of life with grace and love. As we deepen our relationship with Him, we discover a sense of peace and assurance that transcends all understanding. Let us hold fast to our faith in Jesus, for in Him we find true refuge and strength.

Navigating life's challenges can feel like enduring a relentless storm, but faith often acts as a steadfast anchor. It's the belief in something greater than ourselves, offering strength and hope even when the seas are turbulent. Faith doesn't eliminate difficulties, but provides a buoyant perspective, helping us face adversities with courage and a sense of purpose.

In times of uncertainty and hardship, faith can serve as a guiding light, providing comfort and assurance that we are not alone in our struggles. It can instill a sense of peace and resilience, empowering individuals to persevere through even the darkest of times. By cultivating faith, individuals can find solace amid chaos and draw upon inner strength to overcome obstacles.

Faith can foster a sense of community and connection

as individuals with shared beliefs come together to support one another through challenging times. This sense of unity and solidarity can create a network of support that enables individuals to weather the storms of life with grace and perseverance.

Faith is not just a passive belief, but a source of active strength and flexibility that empowers individuals to navigate life's challenges with courage and conviction. It provides a sense of purpose and meaning, guiding individuals through challenging times and inspiring them to keep moving forward, even in the face of adversity.

Whether it's faith in a higher power, a sense of destiny, or simply the conviction that things will improve, it can be a source of immense comfort. Trusting that there is light at the end of the tunnel can transform even the darkest times into opportunities for growth and self-discovery.

# 16

# An Anchor for Renee

M Y WIFE, RENEE, AND I took an exciting trip with a tour group out of Savannah, Georgia, to the beautiful state of Maine a few years ago. Our ten-day trip included several sightseeing stops. We spent three days in beautiful Booth Bay Harbor, Maine, right on the ocean.

Our journey started from Savannah, Georgia, where we boarded the tour bus that would take us on our adventure. The scenic drive through different states was breathtaking, with changing landscapes and charming towns along the way. As we made our way up north, the anticipation of reaching Booth Bay Harbor grew with each passing mile.

Upon arriving in Booth Bay Harbor, the picturesque coastal town mesmerized us. The salty sea breeze, the sound of seagulls, and the sight of lobster boats added to the charm of this quaint destination. Our accommodation was a cozy inn overlooking the harbor, providing us with stunning views of the ocean and the bustling activities of the town.

Our time in Booth Bay Harbor was truly unforgettable, filled with moments of relaxation, exploration, and togetherness. It was a perfect getaway that allowed us to disconnect from the hustle and bustle of everyday life and immerse ourselves in the natural beauty of Maine's coast.

We looked forward to getting our first taste of Maine lobsters. The setting was breathtaking. The rugged coastline, the quaint cottages, the lobster boats in the bay, all added to the beauty of this scenic village when we arrived.

On the first night of our trip, we gathered at a table with our tour guide and fellow travelers, engaging in lively conversations while eagerly expecting our Maine lobster feast. As we donned the bibs recommended by the servers, excitement filled the air. However, the mood took a sharp turn when Renee, after a few bites of her lobster, began experiencing abdominal pain. Concerned, the next morning she sought medical help at a local clinic, where doctors diagnosed her with pancreatitis.

They urgently transferred Renee to the nearest hospital, thirty miles away in Damariscotta, Maine. As her husband,

I rented a car to be by her side during this unexpected turn of events. For the next five days, I made the journey to Damariscotta daily to offer support and comfort to Renee as she navigated through her health ordeal.

After the team departed two days following Renee's attack, I found myself alone at the Inn, making daily trips to the hospital. Despite feeling overwhelmed, a newfound sense of strength propelled me forward. Against all odds, I rent a car and navigate the winding single lane highways of Maine to reach the hospital. The gravity of Renee's condition weighed heavily on my mind, as she had always been my rock - steady, and resolute in times of crisis. She was now an extremely sick lady, and I did all that I could to make her hospital stay as accommodating as possible.

During a challenging time, the Inn generously provided us with a discounted room for three days, understanding our situation. The restaurant staff not only knew me by name but also showed genuine care by inquiring about Renee's well-being at every meal and offering their prayers. Their kindness and support served as a comforting anchor during a difficult period.

The hospital staff were very attentive to Renee's needs. Despite being a smaller facility, the level of care provided was comparable to that of a large metropolitan hospital. Their dedication and professionalism contributed to our positive experience during a trying time.

On Friday afternoon, the staff at the hospital released Renee after her medical check-up. Worried about her, we immediately booked a Delta flight from Portland, Maine to Atlanta, then on to Savannah to get our car. Despite the challenges, we were determined to make it back home to Statesboro, Georgia. The journey was long and arduous, and we arrived home at 3 am, feeling tired, weary, and worn-thin.

The trip had taken a toll on Renee, but it had also been an interesting experience for me. It made me reflect on the importance of resilience and the strength of our bonds. No matter the challenges we face or the distances we travel, our anchor holds firm and guides us back home.

During a boat tour in Booth Bay, I could visit the lighthouses in the area. As the boat approached the rocks jutting out of the bay, I was delighted to see puffins and seals basking in the sun. In addition, I spotted two majestic eagles tending to their nest, a truly breathtaking sight.

After the boat tour, I explored the quaint village of Booth Bay, taking in the charm of its streets and buildings.

I explored the Botanical Garden, a highlight of my visit, immersing myself in colorful flowers and lush greenery. Booth Bay proved to be a delightful destination, offering a mix of natural beauty and cultural experiences. Renee and I vowed to return to Booth Bay in the future to enjoy its beauty.

During that boat tour, I had the privilege of meeting a seasoned lobsterman who generously shared his wealth of knowledge about boating and the process of lobstering. His expertise was truly the highlight of my trip. The lobsterman's understanding of boating was remarkable, as he recounted a harrowing experience of weathering a storm alone in his lobster boat off the coast. Despite the crashing waves and darkness surrounding him, he remained calm, trusting in the strength of his anchor to keep him steady. He emphasized the importance of checking the anchor daily before setting sail, as it is the key to staying grounded and safe amidst the unpredictable waters. The encounter left me in awe of the lobsterman's resilience and wisdom, highlighting the profound bond between a sailor and their vessel.

Just as important as that lobsterman's anchor is to his seafaring, so are we to each other. I was Renee's anchor on our trip when she needed me most. Each of us grounds the other, and we both ground ourselves in God. Our faith sustains us through many situations. We have weathered various storms through the years and have been victorious through them all, for we know who our anchor is!

In life, having someone who serves as an anchor is crucial. Like how a lobsterman relies on his anchor to navigate the rough seas, we lean on each other for support and stability. Through thick and thin, Renee and I have stood by each other, providing strength and comfort when needed the most. Our shared faith in God has been the cornerstone of our relationship, guiding us through the challenges and triumphs we have faced together.

As we journey through life's unpredictable waters, we find solace in knowing that we are each other's anchors. Just like the lobsterman who trusts in his anchor to keep him steady, we place our trust in one another and in our unwavering faith. Together, we have proven repeatedly that with love, support, and faith, we can overcome any storm that comes our way.

—◦❖◦—

# 17

# Anchored in Grace

H EBREWS 6:19: "WHICH HOPE we have as an anchor of the soul, both sure and stedfast, and which
entereth into that within the veil." - Hebrews 6:19

In this verse from the book of Hebrews, the author
uses the powerful metaphor of hope as an anchor for the
soul. Just as a ship's anchor provides stability and security
during turbulent waters, our hope in God serves as a firm
and secure foundation for our lives. This verse reminds us
that no matter what challenges or uncertainties we may
face, we can find strength and peace in the unwavering
hope we have in God. It is a comforting reassurance that
our faith in Him will keep us grounded and steadfast in
the face of life's storms.

Our story revolves around three individuals whose acts
of kindness, bravery, and love are not just driven by good-

will, but firmly rooted in their faith and reliance on God's Word. Their lives intertwine in ways that reveal the transformative power of living by Scripture.

1. **Rachel, the overworked nurse**

People knew Rachel for her dedication to her work at the hospital, where she often volunteered for double shifts to ensure each patient received her special brand of love and care. Her compassion extended beyond the hospital walls, as she helped those in need. A noteworthy instance involved Rachel assisting a homeless man, embodying the principles of Matthew 25:40: "Truly, I tell you, whatever you did for one of the least of these brothers and sisters of mine, you did for me."

Rachel, exhausted from a long day, was making her way back home when she came across a homeless man in need. Despite her fatigue, her compassionate nature compelled her to stop and assist him. Without hesitation, she called the hospital, and they promptly dispatched an ambulance to aid the man.

Weeks later, the same homeless man arrived at the hospital emergency room where Rachel worked. Overwhelmed with gratitude, he embraced her and expressed his heartfelt thanks for her timely intervention. In that moment,

Rachel realized that her swift actions had not only helped the man in need but had also saved his life.

### 2. **Larry, the retired firefighter**

As he works tirelessly to repair the church one day, Larry begins to meditate on Psalm 46:1—"God is our refuge and strength, an ever-present help in trouble." His actions reflect his reliance on God's strength to rebuild not just the church, but his sense of purpose. Amidst the broken walls and crumbling pillars, he finds solace in the words of scripture, drawing inspiration from the promise of divine support and guidance.

With each brick he lays and every beam he reinforces, he pours his faith into the restoration process, believing that through his hands, God's work is being done. This journey of rebuilding transcends mere physical reconstruction; it symbolizes a spiritual renewal, a testament to his steadfast trust in God's provision and protection. Through the debris and challenges, his unwavering faith serves as a beacon of hope, illuminating the path towards a brighter future for both the church and his own soul.

### 3. **Ariana, the young teacher**

Faced with criticism for welcoming refugee children, Ariana finds solace in the words of Galatians 6:9, which states, "Let us not become weary in doing good, for at the proper time we will reap a harvest if we do not give up." This biblical verse serves as a source of strength and inspiration for Ariana, reminding her to persevere in her compassionate actions despite opposition.

Her unwavering courage and commitment to helping others not only reflect her deep faith but also inspire those around her to seek guidance from the Word of God in times of challenge and uncertainty. Through her actions, Ariana exemplifies the power of faith and kindness in making a positive impact on the world.

Tested faith and a desperate need for hope define a small town where a group of characters learns the life-changing power of anchoring themselves to their religious beliefs, finding strength and resilience in the Word.

Characters:

1. Helen: A young woman who finds solace in scripture during times of trouble.

2. Herman: A pastor who leads by example, showing the importance of faith in action.

3. Christy: an elderly widow whose unwavering belief in God's promises inspires others.

4. Earnest: Those around him transformed the skeptic

with their faith and kindness.

Grace is the operative word for each of these situations. It is the grace of God that saves us; we do not save ourselves. "Anchored in Grace" is a story of hope, faith, and the enduring power of God's promises. It reminds us that in times of uncertainty, turning to scripture and relying on our faith can not only sustain us but also uplift those around us.

In a world filled with challenges and uncertainties, the concept of grace serves as a beacon of light, guiding us through the darkest of times. It is through the grace of God that we find salvation and redemption, offering a sense of peace and comfort amidst the storms of life. "Anchored in Grace" beautifully illustrates the transformative power of faith and the steadfast love that God provides to His children.

This story guides readers through a journey of self-discovery and spiritual growth as they witness the characters' enduring faith while facing trials and tribulations. The narrative serves as a poignant reminder that no matter the circumstances we face, God's grace suffices to carry us through.

The narrative of "Anchored in Grace" encourages us to

reflect on our own lives and how faith shapes our perspectives and guides our actions. It is a testament to the enduring power of God's promises and the transformative impact that His grace can have on our lives. This story inspires us to embrace grace as a guiding principle, anchoring ourselves in God's steadfast love.

Our journey of faith reminds us not to grow weary in doing good, for many among us face challenges beyond our understanding. As followers of Jesus Christ, it is our responsibility to seek opportunities to be the physical embodiment of His love and compassion. Through our actions, words, and deeds, we can serve as instruments of grace and hope in a world that is often filled with despair. Let us remember that grace saved us, and we must share this gift with others, leading them to God's transformative love.

# 18

# An Anchor in the Wilderness

I N LUKE 4:1-13, THE narrative unfolds with Jesus experiencing a moment of elation following his baptism by John in the river Jordan. However, this joyous occasion quickly transitions as the Holy Spirit leads him into the wilderness for a period of intense testing. In this arduous trial, Jesus faces a series of temptations presented by the devil himself. Jesus resolutely relied on God's word to overcome temptation, even in difficult circumstances. This powerful example guides believers during trials and spiritual battles. Luke's account powerfully shows Jesus' strength and unwavering commitment to his mission, even amidst adversity. This highlights Jesus' divine nature.

The metaphor of the wilderness, a place of desolation and challenges, is a space of testing and transformation. In thinking on the story, I wanted us to look at Jesus' responses in serving as an anchor for us in our own times of wilderness and temptation. Part One is the setting of the Wilderness. The Wilderness contains solitude and vulnerability. These mirror the trials we face in life: moments of uncertainty, isolation, or inner struggle. The 40 days Jesus spent in the wilderness represent both a physical challenge and spiritual preparation.

The wilderness, with its barren landscapes and harsh conditions, serves as a metaphor for the challenging times we encounter in life. Just as Jesus faced temptation and testing during his time in the wilderness, we, too, face challenges that test our faith and character. The solitude and vulnerability of the wilderness reflect the moments of uncertainty and isolation we experience in our own lives. These struggles transform and refine us, much like Jesus' experience, during his 40 days in the wilderness.

Solo mountain trips have always been refreshing, especially during my ministry years. They provided time for reflection and renewal. Alone with God, I could see how vast and important everything was, and how insignificant I was in comparison.

Towering peaks, whispering winds, and a vast expanse of nature reminded me of the world's magnificence. Taking a step back to appreciate it is important.

In those moments of solitude, I found clarity, peace, and a renewed sense of purpose that helped me navigate the challenges of my work and life with a fresh perspective. The mountains became my sanctuary, a place where I could disconnect from the noise of the world and reconnect with my inner self and spiritual beliefs.

I'm continually inspired by the memories of my solitary mountain excursions, which highlight nature's and solitude's positive effects on my well-being and spiritual growth. I still yearn for those times as I age.

The first temptation is **Turning Stones to Bread**.

This temptation is about our physical needs and desires. There is always the temptation for us to prioritize physical needs over spiritual reliance. When Jesus said, "Man shall not live by bread alone", he is pointing to the deeper nourishment found in God's Word.

The second temptation is that of **Kingdoms and Glory**.

This temptation challenges us to prioritize our material needs over our spiritual well-being. As a minister, this could serve as a powerful three-point sermon to remind the congregation about staying true to their faith in the face of worldly temptations.

The third temptation is **Leaping from the Temple.**

Testing God refers to the act of seeking sensational proof of God's power. This temptation often arises from a desire to manipulate God's promises for personal gain or validation. However, Jesus teaches a different approach - one that emphasizes trust with no testing. By refusing to engage in manipulative practices or seek dramatic displays of divine power, Jesus underscores the importance of genuine faith and belief in God's promises. This principle serves as a reminder to approach spirituality with humility, reverence, and trust in the unseen, rather than seeking external validations or proofs.

Jesus anchors himself through scripture, countering every temptation with the truth of God's Word. He anchors himself through faithful dependence on God, trusting in God's plan over immediate gratification or worldly solutions. He also anchors himself through the power of the Holy Spirit. Note, if you will, that Jesus entered and left the wilderness "filled with the Spirit" (Luke 4:1, 14).

I invite you to reflect on how these same anchors of Scripture, Faith, and the Spirit, can sustain you in your own wilderness experiences.

Jesus' responses teach us to rely on God's Word, remain faithful, and use the Holy Spirit's power during struggles and temptations.

The Bible frequently portrays the wilderness as a place of testing and transformation, where trials shape individuals' faith and character. One notable example is the experience of the Israelites, who wandered in the wilderness for 40 years, a period marked by both challenges and divine provision (Exodus 16:4).

Isolation and vulnerability are symbolized by the wilderness, where the wilderness strips individuals of familiar comforts, leaving them to rely solely on their faith in God. The Bible shows Moses, Elijah, and Jesus, among others, spending time in the wilderness to prepare for their divine callings.

The wilderness is often associated with purification and renewal. In the New Testament, John the Baptist preached in the wilderness, calling people to repentance and baptism to prepare for the coming of the Messiah. The harsh, barren landscape of the wilderness provides a backdrop for spiritual growth and renewal, stripping individuals of distractions and worldly influences.

The wilderness plays a significant role in the Bible as

a setting for testing, transformation, and renewal. The wilderness confronts individuals with their limitations and vulnerabilities; however, it also allows them profoundly to experience God's presence and provision. Believers find comfort and strength in God's presence during challenging times. He guides them and strengthens their faith. Symbolically, the wilderness represents periods in our lives when we face uncertainty, hardship, or temptation. These moments test our reliance on God and refine our trust in His guidance.

The wilderness is not just a place of hardship, but also one of growth and preparation. It serves as a transformative space where individuals can fortify their purpose and resist external challenges. For Jesus, the wilderness was a prelude to His public ministry, providing a crucial time for Him to strengthen His mission and confront the adversary's tactics. Spiritually, the wilderness symbolizes the transitional phases in life - periods of waiting or change that lead to personal growth and rejuvenation. Just as Jesus emerged from the wilderness ready to embark on His divine calling, individuals can emerge from their own wilderness experiences transformed and renewed.

In the wilderness, there are few distractions. It is a place where one must confront themselves and their relationship with God. This solitude can be daunting but also deeply clarifying, as it forces a focus on inner strength and divine dependence.

In my first appointment as a pastor, I would spend about an hour each Sunday morning in the local city cemetery praying and preparing the last touches to my sermon for the day. I cherished those moments of solitude, knowing I would be undisturbed.

Paradoxically, the wilderness is often the setting for profound encounters with God. Throughout history, various spiritual figures have experienced divine revelations in the desolate expanses of nature. One notable example is Moses, who encountered the burning bush and received a divine calling to lead the Israelites out of Egypt (Exodus 3). Similarly, the prophet Elijah heard the whisper of God amidst the solitude and chaos of the wilderness, finding reassurance and guidance in his moment of despair (I Kings 19:12).

In these remote and barren landscapes, God becomes unmistakably clear, transcending the distractions of daily life. The wilderness also serves as a metaphor for our internal struggles and spiritual battles. It symbolizes the doubts, fears, and temptations that we face in our journey towards spiritual growth and enlightenment.

Drawing inspiration from Jesus' own wilderness experience, where He overcame temptation and emerged spiritually strengthened (Matthew 4:1-11), we can find solace and strength in our own moments of struggle. Just as the wilderness can be a place of profound encounters with the divine, it can also be a space for personal reflection, growth, and transformation.

Modern day "wilderness" experiences may not involve physical deserts or isolation, but they represent periods of challenge. Let me mention just a few.

**Personal Crisis**: Losing a job, going through a divorce, or facing a health scare can feel like being lost in a wilderness.

**Periods of Waiting**: Waiting for a breakthrough, whether in career, relationships, or personal goals, can feel like wandering in the wilderness. We often find our patience tested.

**Spiritual Dryness**: Feeling distant from God or struggling with doubt can be a wilderness experience. It's a time when prayer feels distant and difficult, and one might feel spiritually "lost" or disconnected.

**Major Life Transitions**: Moving to a new city, changing careers, or entering a new phase of life (like retirement or becoming a parent) can feel overwhelming, like stepping into the unknown.

**Grief and Loss**: The loss of a loved one can leave individuals in a state of emotional wilderness, grappling with sorrow, and searching for meaning.

**Moral or Ethical Dilemmas**: Facing tough decisions that test one's values can feel like a wilderness moment, where the right path may not be immediately clear.

**Global or Societal Challenges**: Events like a pandemic, economic downturn, or social unrest can create collective wilderness experiences, where communities face uncertainty and must rely on resilience and unity.

These experiences, while difficult, can also be life changing. They often lead to growth, a deeper understanding of oneself, and a renewed sense of purpose.

God bless you on your journey today.

# 19

# Grace: The Invisible Anchor

N THE UNPREDICTABLE SEAS of life, we all experience
moments when the waters rise, the winds howl, and
we fear being pulled under. In these moments, an anchor is
essential—something that holds us firm amidst the chaos,
steadying us when the world feels out of control. For those
walking in faith, that anchor is God's grace, unseen yet
undeniably powerful. We receive grace freely; it is a gift
we haven't earned and don't deserve. It operates quietly,
often unnoticed, yet its impact is profound. Unlike material anchors, things we strive to achieve or gain, grace is
a divine constant that neither diminishes nor wavers. It is
there, holding us, even when we feel unmoored, lost, or
undeserving.

Through the storms of life, God's grace serves as the
unwavering anchor that keeps us grounded. It provides a

sense of stability and assurance when everything around us seems turbulent and uncertain. By relying on this divine gift, we can find strength and resilience to weather life's challenges with faith and courage. God's grace is a reminder that we are never alone, even in our darkest moments, as it offers a sense of comfort and hope that transcends human understanding. Faith provides peace and trust during life's uncertainties. It's an unseen anchor guiding and protecting us.

In a pivotal moment of my life, grace ceased to be a mere concept and transformed into a lifeline that sustained me through tumultuous times. I found myself engulfed in a season of uncertainty and doubt, feeling like a ship lost in a relentless storm with no end in sight.

Despite my relentless efforts to regain control, peace seemed to slip further away from my grasp with each passing day. Desperate, I turned to scripture. I found 2 Corinthians 12:9: "My grace is sufficient for thee: for my strength is made perfect in weakness." I realized my strength was not the solution to my struggles; rather, it was in placing my trust in the unwavering grace of God.

From that moment of epiphany, a subtle yet profound shift occurred within me. I no longer felt alone amid life's challenges. It was as if an invisible force was guiding me, offering a sense of reassurance that transcended the storm raging around me. Grace, in its mysterious and miraculous ways, gently steered me back to a place of inner peace, providing a constant reminder that I was never alone in my journey.

Grace helped me find resilience and faith to overcome any future challenges. I believe its unwavering presence will always sustain me.

Grace meets us in our failures, transforming our weakness into strength. It lifts us when we stumble, reminding us that His love is not contingent on our perfection. Grace whispers to us in our darkest moments, assuring us that no matter how far we drift, we are never beyond His reach.

In embracing grace, I found solace and strength to navigate the uncertainties of life. It became a beacon of hope in times of despair and a source of steadfast support in moments of doubt. Through the lens of grace, I learned to see setbacks as opportunities for growth and challenges as steppingstones towards personal development.

Grace has been my guiding light, providing me with the courage to face life's obstacles and the wisdom to find meaning in every experience. It has taught me the power of forgiveness, both towards others and myself, and the importance of cultivating compassion and empathy in all interactions. With grace as my compass, I have embraced a mindset of gratitude and acceptance, allowing me to find peace amidst life's storms.

As I continue this journey of self-discovery and growth, I am grateful for the transformative power of grace in my life. It has enabled me to find strength in vulnerability, to seek beauty in imperfection, and to embrace the fullness of my humanity. Through grace, I have learned that true resilience lies not in avoiding challenges but in facing them with an open heart and a steadfast spirit.

In moments of doubt or darkness, grace has been a beacon of hope, reminding me of the inherent goodness that lives within me and every individual. It has shown me that growth is not always linear but a messy, nonlinear process filled with twists and turns.

Through grace, I have embraced the ebb and flow of life, finding peace amid chaos and joy in the simplest of moments. As I reflect on the impact of grace in my life, I am filled with gratitude for its steadfast presence and transformative influence. It has been a catalyst for profound personal growth and a source of inspiration as I navigate the complexities of existence. With grace as my guide, I walk forward with confidence, knowing that I am supported, cherished, and infinitely loved.

Grace has been my steadfast companion, offering solace and strength during times of uncertainty. Its gentle touch has guided me through challenges and setbacks, teaching me resilience and perseverance. I have learned to embrace imperfections and setbacks as opportunities for growth, trusting in the process of life's unfolding journey. Through grace, I have discovered a deep sense of inner peace and acceptance, allowing me to approach each day with a renewed sense of purpose and gratitude.

As I continue to walk the path illuminated by grace, I am reminded of the interconnectedness of all beings and the power of compassion and empathy. Grace has taught me the importance of kindness, forgiveness, and understanding in cultivating harmonious relationships and fostering a sense of community. It has shown me that true strength lies in vulnerability and authenticity, encouraging me to embrace my true self and share my light with the world.

In conclusion, grace has been a guiding light in my life, leading me towards self-discovery, resilience, and a deeper connection with the world around me. Its transformative influence has shaped my perspective and empowered me to navigate life's challenges with grace and courage. With gratitude in my heart, I embrace the journey ahead, knowing that I am supported by the unwavering presence of grace.

This conversation highlights Grace's profound impact on my life. It shapes my perspective, guides my actions, and illuminates my path to purpose and fulfillment.

I'm on a journey guided by grace. This means knowing I'm never alone, that I'm worthy of love and forgiveness, and that divine guidance leads me toward purpose. I am finding fulfillment along the way. Grace has transformed my perspective, empowered my spirit, and illuminated my path with a radiance that can only come from embracing the boundless love and compassion of the divine.

Like the anchor that holds a ship steadfast against the wind and currents, grace keeps our spiritual foundation firm. It encourages us to forgive, both others and ourselves, breaking free from the chains of anger, resentment, and regret that weigh us down. And it emboldens us to face challenges with courage, knowing we are not walking alone.

As you consider the invisible anchor of grace in your

own life, reflect on the ways it has held you steady through challenges. Let this serve as a reminder that who you are is not determined by past errors and that your anxieties or uncertainties do not constrain your potential. A God who never lets go reminds us of his love, redemption, and resolute support.

# 20

# Anchored through Divine Encounters

THERE ARE MOMENTS IN life when the noise of the world grows overwhelming—when the clamor of doubt, fear, and uncertainty drowns out all clarity. For Francis, a single mother juggling a demanding job and the responsibilities of raising two children, this noise had reached its peak. The weight of financial struggles and the loneliness of her journey left her feeling like a ship adrift, far from the safety of any shore.

Desperate for guidance, Francis turned to prayer one evening. It wasn't a grand or formal prayer; it was raw and unfiltered words spoken with a trembling voice in the solitude of her room. "God, I don't know what to do," she whispered through tears, "but I can't keep going like this." She sat there in silence, expecting nothing, yet hoping for everything. And in that stillness, something extraordinary happened. A profound sense of peace washed over her—a warmth that enveloped her heart. It wasn't an external voice, but an internal knowing, a whisper within her soul: "You are not alone. Trust, and take the next step."

In that moment of vulnerability and surrender, Francis found solace. The weight that had burdened her for so long lifted, replaced by a newfound sense of assurance.

The journey ahead remained uncertain, but she embraced it with a renewed spirit. This experience taught her the power of faith, the beauty of seeking comfort amid chaos, and the importance of listening to the whispers of the soul. Francis emerged from that night with a strengthened resolve and a deep-seated belief that, no matter the challenges she faced, she was never truly alone.

I remember a time in my life when prayer became a lifeline. It was during a season of uncertainty, much like Francis's. I've seen how moments of silent, heartfelt connection with God have transformed countless lives. Prayer can provide solace, guidance, and strength during challenging times. It serves as a beacon of hope and a source of comfort for many individuals facing uncertainties in their lives. Through prayer, people find a sense of peace, clarity, and resilience to navigate through difficult circumstances. It is a powerful tool that can bring about inner peace and a renewed sense of faith in times of distress.

One individual I've learned about shared how they prayed for clarity while navigating a career shift. They described how, after weeks of feeling unheard and uncertain about their future, they sought solace in prayer and meditation. Through moments of stillness and deep reflection, they poured their heart out, seeking guidance and purpose. And then, one fateful morning, they awoke with an unshakable idea—a vision that was given to them by a higher power.

This inspired plan was to start a nonprofit organization, a venture fueled by passion and a desire to make a positive impact in the world. Despite initial doubts and fears, the individual felt a sense of certainty and purpose unlike anything they had experienced before. As they stood at the beginning of a path, which was now illuminated before them, a new journey unfolded, inviting them to embark on an adventure filled with the unknown.

As they poured their energy and dedication into building the nonprofit, they witnessed it flourish beyond their wildest dreams. The impact it had on the community and

the lives it touched were a testament to the divine intervention that guided their steps. For them, this encounter was
not just a stroke of luck or a coincidence—it was a gift born
of faith, perseverance, and determined belief in something
greater than themselves.

Through this experience, they learned the power of
faith, prayer, and listening to the whispers of the universe.
It taught them to trust, to embrace uncertainty, and to
have faith that the answers will reveal themselves in time.
This individual's story serves as a reminder that sometimes, the most profound clarity and inspiration can come
from moments of stillness, when we allow ourselves to be
open to the guidance of something beyond our comprehension.

Here are some thoughtful reflection prompts for you to
connect deeply with this message and story:

**Personal Prayer Experience**

Have you ever turned to prayer during a challenging
time? What emotions did you experience, and did you find
any clarity or peace afterward?

During challenging times in my life, I have often turned
to prayer as a source of comfort and guidance. The emotions I experienced while praying ranged from fear and

uncertainty to hope and trust. Through prayer, I found a sense of clarity and peace that helped me navigate through demanding situations. The act of praying allowed me to express my innermost feelings and concerns, and in return, I felt a sense of relief and assurance that I was not alone in facing my struggles.

Prayer provided me with a sense of connection to something greater than myself and helped me find strength and resilience to overcome obstacles. Overall, my personal prayer experiences have been transformative, helping me find solace and peace amidst life's challenges.

**Moments of Silence**

Moments of silence hold immense power in our fast-paced world, providing us with an opportunity to pause, reflect, and connect with our inner thoughts. When was the last time you truly sat in silence and reflected? How did that moment shape your thoughts or actions?

The last time I experienced a moment of silence was last year during a solo hike in the mountains. As I reached a serene spot overlooking a breathtaking view, I sat down and soaked in the surrounding tranquility. With no distractions, I closed my eyes and let my mind roam. In that moment of stillness, I could process recent events, gain clarity on my priorities, and appreciate the beauty of nature. This reflection helped me realign my thoughts and actions, leading me to make some important decisions regarding my personal and professional life.

Taking the time to sit in silence and reflect can have a profound impact on our mental and emotional well-being. It allows us to gain perspective, make sense of our experiences, and find inner peace. The next time you find yourself caught up in the chaos of daily life, remember the power of moments of silence and the positive influence they can have on your thoughts and actions.

**Hearing God's Voice**

Have you ever experienced the sense of God speaking to you, whether through a thought, feeling, or event? This profound experience has the power to influence our decisions and shape our perspectives in significant ways.

There are many ways in which people may feel they have heard God's voice in their lives. Some may describe it as a sudden clarity of thought that guides them towards a particular direction. Others may feel a deep sense of peace or assurance in their hearts when faced with a hard decision. Others may attribute certain events or encounters as divine interventions that have led them on a specific path.

Regardless of the form it takes, the influence of hearing God's voice can be profound. It can provide clarity in times of confusion, comfort in moments of distress, and courage in the face of fear. It can also challenge our preconceived notions and push us out of our comfort zones towards growth and transformation.

The experience of hearing God's voice is a deeply personal and spiritual one that can have a lasting impact on our lives. By being attuned to these moments of divine communication, we can navigate life's challenges with faith and confidence, knowing that we are being guided by a higher power.

### Faith in Difficult Times

Think of a time when life felt overwhelming. How did your faith (or search for faith) help you navigate that season?

During a challenging period in my life, when I felt overwhelmed by various personal and professional struggles, my faith played a crucial role in helping me navigate through the storm. I turned to prayer and meditation to find solace and strength in the face of adversity. Through my faith, I could cultivate a sense of hope and resilience that helped me endure difficult circumstances. It provided me with a sense of purpose and a belief that there was a higher power guiding me through the challenges I was facing. My faith served as a beacon of light in the darkness, offering me comfort, courage, and a renewed sense of perspective during that trying season.

### The Role of Prayer in Your Life

Prayer is a powerful practice that holds significance in the lives of many individuals, providing a means of connection with the divine or spiritual realm. How does prayer currently fit into your daily life?

Prayer plays a vital role in shaping our daily routines and providing a source of solace, guidance, and reflection. By taking the time to engage in prayer regularly, we invite a sense of peace and mindfulness into our lives.

However, it is essential to reflect on how we can enhance our connection through prayer or meditation. This may involve setting aside dedicated time each day for prayer, exploring different prayer practices or rituals, or seeking guidance from spiritual leaders or mentors. By deepening our connection through prayer, we can cultivate a more profound sense of spiritual awareness and presence in our daily lives.

Prayer serves as a vital component of our spiritual

well-being and personal growth. By reflecting on how prayer currently fits into our daily lives and exploring ways to deepen our connection through prayer or meditation, we can nurture a stronger sense of connection with the divine and cultivate a more profound spiritual practice.

## Finding Strength in Vulnerability

Francis's story beautifully exemplifies the transformative power of honest and vulnerable prayer. It highlights how opening up and expressing raw emotions and fears can lead to healing and growth. This narrative resonates with many individuals who have experienced the cathartic release that comes with sharing vulnerabilities. We should explore the significance of embracing vulnerability in prayer and in conversations with trusted individuals.

Expressing raw emotions and fears in prayer or to a trusted person can be a deeply personal and profound experience. It requires a willingness to be transparent and authentic, allowing oneself to be seen in a raw and unfiltered state. This act of vulnerability can create a sense of connection, both with oneself and with others. It opens the door to empathy, understanding, and support, fostering a deeper sense of intimacy and trust in relationships.

Sharing vulnerabilities in prayer can also be surrender, a

letting go of control and a recognition of our limitations. It is an acknowledgment of our humanity and a humble plea for guidance and strength. Baring our souls to a higher power, we invite grace and compassion into our lives, finding solace in the belief that we are not alone in our struggles.

Similarly, confiding in a trusted person can provide a sense of relief and comfort. Confiding in a trusted person creates a space where empathy replaces judgment, compassion meets fears, and understanding supports vulnerabilities. The act of sharing our innermost thoughts and feelings with another person can be a powerful act of courage and trust, deepening bonds and fostering a sense of community.

In a world that often values strength and stoicism, embracing vulnerability can be a radical act of self-love and resilience. Olivia's story serves as a reminder of the beauty and power that comes from allowing ourselves to be seen and heard in our most authentic and vulnerable state. Whether through prayer or through conversations with trusted individuals, expressing raw emotions and fears can lead to profound healing, connection, and growth. It is through vulnerability that we find strength, courage, and the steadfast support of those who genuinely care for us.

**Recognizing Divine Encounters**

Have you ever experienced a moment of profound peace, guidance, or blessing that felt like a divine encounter? These encounters can come in various forms - a gentle whisper in your heart, a sense of overwhelming peace amid chaos, or a serendipitous meeting that feels like more than just a coincidence.

These moments often leave us in awe of the mysterious ways in which the divine can manifest in our lives. They can be a source of comfort, inspiration, and reassurance, reminding us we are not alone and that there is a higher power watching over us. Reflecting on these encounters can deepen our faith and strengthen our connection to the divine, changing our view of God's presence in our lives from abstract belief to tangible experience. Have you had a divine encounter that left a lasting impact on you?

**Taking the Next Step**

Today, I feel called to take a small step towards addressing my struggle of procrastination. I plan to start by creating a daily to-do list with specific tasks and deadlines to hold myself accountable. I believe that by breaking down my goals into manageable steps and staying committed to my plan, I can overcome this challenge and make progress towards achieving my objectives.

In this journey, my faith will support me by providing me with the strength and determination to stay focused and persevere, even when faced with obstacles. I will trust in the guidance and support that my faith offers, helping me to stay motivated and confident in my ability to overcome any challenges that come my way.

May these prompts encourage you to reflect on your own spiritual journeys and even foster a sense of hope and connection.

# 21

# The Symbolic Anchor

F OR A LONG TIME, people have considered anchors powerful symbols that transcend their practical maritime use. People often see them as representations of hope, providing a sense of security amidst uncertainty. Early Christians recognized anchors as disguised symbols of the cross, symbolizing faith and hope during times of persecution. In art and literature, anchors consistently convey the concepts of steadfastness and a secure, grounded existence, highlighting the importance of resilience in navigating life's challenges.

Within the realm of tattoo culture, the anchor design holds significant symbolic meaning, representing a deep connection to the sea or an individual's unwavering resilience in the face of adversity. Despite life's unpredictability, people wear anchor tattoos as a reminder to remain grounded and steadfast. Beyond personal interpretations, anchors carry a broader metaphorical significance, often used in motivational speeches to underscore the importance of stability and support during challenging times.

The enduring appeal of anchors lies in their ability to resonate with people's core values, whether derived from family, faith, or personal passions. Anchors serve as reminders to stay resilient and grounded in the face of life's challenges, embodying the universal message of perseverance and unwavering strength.

Let's delve deeper into the cultural and literary uses of anchor symbolism.

**Anchor Symbolism in Literature**

**Classical and Religious Texts:**

Early Christian texts portray anchors as a secret symbol of faith and hope. The "Epistle to the Hebrews" in the Bible notably likens hope to "an anchor for the soul, firm and secure" (Hebrews 6:19). The metaphor highlights the crucial need for unwavering resolve and steadfastness on one's spiritual journey. Facing challenges requires this essential quality. Anchors powerfully symbolize steadfast faith and enduring hope, essential Christian virtues offering stability and security during life's challenges. This symbolism continues to resonate within Christian teachings, illustrating the importance of standing strong in one's beliefs regardless of the challenges faced.

**Poetry:**

In poetry, anchors often symbolize emotional stability or the weight of responsibility. For instance, 19th- and 20th-century poets frequently used anchors to depict a grounding force amidst turbulent emotions or existential drift. Various poetic works use this symbolism, using anchors metaphorically to convey security, resilience, and steadfastness against adversity. By incorporating anchors into their verses, poets evoke themes of stability, endurance, and the ability to weather life's storms.

The imagery of an anchor holding firm amid chaos resonates with readers, offering a sense of hope and reassurance in uncertain times. Using anchors in poetry, writers explore the complexities of human emotions and the quest for inner strength and stability.

**Fiction and novels:**

Sea-themed novels frequently use anchors as powerful symbols, drawing upon their dual roles as both literal tools and metaphorical devices. Herman Melville's

"Moby-Dick" offers a prime example, portraying anchors as more than simple ship-securing devices. Instead,
Melville gives the anchors deeper meanings—symbolizing safety, the connection between humanity and the vast
ocean, and the weight of past deeds. Through these rich
and multifaceted representations, anchors in sea-themed
literature enhance themes of adventure, struggle, and the
enduring relationship between individuals and the sea.

**Anchor Symbolism in Different Cultures:**

**Maritime Communities:**

Anchors have long held a revered status in coastal cultures worldwide, symbolizing safety and homecoming.
For sailors, an anchor is more than just a tool for securing
a vessel—it represents a safe harbor and a connection to
home. This sentiment is deeply ingrained in maritime traditions, where the presence of an anchor is often associated
with feelings of security and comfort.

Throughout history, anchors have played a crucial role
in the lives of sailors and coastal communities. The sight
of an anchor was a welcome symbol for seafarers returning from long and perilous journeys, signifying the end
of their voyage and the safety of their home port. Many
cultures see anchors as protective talismans that ward off

evil spirits and ensure safe passage for ships at sea.

The design of anchors varies across different regions, reflecting the unique cultural beliefs and practices of coastal communities. People decorate some anchors intricately with symbols and motifs that hold specific meanings, while others bear inscriptions or engravings reminding them of loved ones lost. Regardless of their design, anchors universally evoke feelings of security, stability, and a sense of belonging.

Anchors hold a special place in the hearts of coastal cultures around the world. As symbols of safety and homecoming, they serve as powerful reminders of the enduring connection between sailors and the sea. Anchors evoke nostalgia for maritime traditions. Whether on a ship's bow or in a seaside town, they remind us of our history with the sea.

**Tattoo Culture:**

Anchors have a rich history as one of the oldest and most enduring tattoo symbols. Dating back to the days of sailors, these individuals would often tattoo anchors on their bodies as a symbol of their seafaring experience and as a talisman for safe journeys. This tradition has carried on into modern times, where anchors in tattoos continue to hold significant meaning. Beyond their nautical roots, anchors are a representation of strength, stability, and a deep connection to one's origins. The anchor tattoo remains a timeless and powerful symbol in the world of body art, embodying various qualities that resonate with individuals seeking to express themselves through ink.

**Wider Pop Culture:**

Anchors, originally associated with maritime activities, have developed beyond their nautical roots to become prevalent in various aspects of contemporary society. Because anchors symbolize resilience, reliability, and hope, designers and audiences alike frequently incorporate them into logos, fashion designs, and artwork as powerful and evocative symbols. Their representation has transcended their original meaning, now universally recognized as icons of stability and perseverance. Through their versatile application, anchors have become powerful visual symbols.

Hebrews 6:19, a Bible verse, states: "We have this hope as an anchor for the soul, firm and secure." Just as an anchor holds a ship steady amidst turbulent waters, faith can provide individuals with a sense of grounding and resilience during challenging times. The imagery of an anchor in Hebrews 6:19 serves as a powerful reminder of the strength and steadfastness that faith can offer in navigating the uncertainties of life. They convey messages of strength and determination in today's culture.

Have you discovered that anchor for your soul? A strong anchor is essential for providing stability and strength amid life's storms. It serves as a source of security and grounding, helping you navigate through challenges and uncertainties. Finding this anchor requires introspection, self-awareness, and a deep understanding of your values, beliefs, and purpose. It may come as faith, relationships, personal growth, or a combination of these elements. Once you have found your anchor, nurture it, cherish it, and let it guide you through the highs and lows of life.

# 22

# The Ethereal Dream Weaver

I N A WORLD WHERE dreams and reality intertwine, Lloyd, a weary traveler, finds himself lost in a dense fog that blankets his existence. Exhausted from the weight of his struggles, he stumbles upon an ancient, shimmering archway marked with intricate patterns that seem alive. Beyond it lies a vast, ethereal realm—a place of endless twilight where the stars pulse gently, as if breathing.

A mysterious figure appears, cloaked in gossamer light. They introduce themselves as the Dream Weaver, a guide for those searching for freedom from their burdens. The Weaver offers Lloyd a journey—not to escape his life, but to transcend the fear and pain that bind him. Together, they flew through skies of liquid gold, reviving memories Lloyd thought lost. He revisits moments of joy, love, and courage he had long forgotten, realizing that these fragments of light hold the key to his inner strength.

In this enchanting realm, Lloyd learns to embrace his past and see it not as a chain but as a source of power. The Dream Weaver gently nudges him to confront his deepest fears and doubts, guiding him through trials that test his resolve. Through these challenges, Lloyd discovers hidden reserves of resilience and wisdom within himself. As he sheds the cloak of self-doubt and embraces his true essence, the fog that once clouded his vision lifts, revealing a path illuminated by his newfound inner light.

With the Dream Weaver by his side, Lloyd embarks on a transformative journey of self-discovery and growth. Together, they navigate the ethereal realm, unraveling the threads of his past and weaving them into a tapestry of strength and purpose. Through moments of reflection and introspection, Lloyd finds clarity and peace, understanding that his struggles have shaped him into the resilient soul he is today.

As the journey unfolds, Lloyd realizes that true freedom lies not in escaping his past, but in embracing it wholeheartedly. With the guidance of the Dream Weaver, he learns to dance between dreams and reality, finding harmony in the intricate patterns of his existence. Emerging from the ethereal realm, a renewed sense of purpose and inner peace filled his heart. Hope and possibility radiated from him.

As the journey unfolds, Lloyd learns that the fog he once feared was his own doubt clouding the path forward. The Dream Weaver doesn't deliver salvation but empowers Lloyd to embrace his resilience and navigate life with hope and clarity. When he awakens, the fog has lifted—not in the world around him, but within his soul. Lloyd's transformative experience taught him that true strength lies in self-acceptance. This led to a deeper understanding of himself and the world.

As Lloyd and the Dream Weaver ventured further into the celestial expanse, the landscapes morphed, shifting to reflect fragments of Lloyd's subconscious. They stood atop a cliff bathed in moonlight, overlooking an ocean of glowing memories. The shimmering moonlight cast a surreal glow on the memories below, creating a hauntingly beautiful scene. At other moments, they traversed forests where the trees whispered echoes of his past mistakes and triumphs; the rustling leaves carrying fragments of forgotten conversations and lost dreams.

The Dream Weaver's presence was both calming and

enigmatic, their form ethereal yet reassuring. They spoke in riddles that Lloyd found himself compelled to decipher, each cryptic message revealing a deeper layer of his own psyche. One question lingered persistently in Lloyd's mind: "Am I truly awake, or is this still a dream?" The Weaver turned to him, their radiant light shimmering like liquid starlight against the cosmic backdrop.

"Dreams and reality are threads of the same tapestry," the Dream Weaver intoned, their voice resonating with cosmic wisdom. "Your fear binds you in both worlds. Courage frees you from soul-entangling illusions." Lloyd felt a surge of understanding, as if the cosmos revealed secrets of his being. In that moment, he knew this journey was not just a physical odyssey but a profound exploration of his inner self, guided by the enigmatic presence of the Dream Weaver.

Guided by the Weaver's words, Lloyd faced his greatest fear—a shadowy figure at the center of a swirling void. The figure mirrored every move he made, as though taunting him. Summoning his strength, Lloyd stepped forward and embraced the shadow, acknowledging it as a part of himself.

In that moment, the void transformed into a kaleidoscope of colors. The shadow dissolved, leaving behind a single glowing thread that Lloyd wove into his heart. He felt lighter, stronger—no longer burdened by the weight of his doubts.

The Dream Weaver smiled. "You have found the key to your own freedom," they said. "I am merely the guide; the true power lies within you."

As Lloyd basked in the clarity of his newfound strength, a sharp, chilling wind swept through the dreamscape. As the once vibrant kaleidoscope of colors dimmed, the Dream Weaver, with flickering, shimmering light, turned toward the horizon. "The journey is not yet over," they said, their voice heavy with an unspoken truth. The sky fractured, revealing a void darker than anything Lloyd had ever seen. From the void emerged a second figure—a perfect doppelgänger of Lloyd, except their eyes burned with anguish and resentment. "You've found strength," the figure said with a bitter sneer, "but what of the pain you left behind?"

In this surreal dreamscape, Lloyd faces a mirror image of himself that questions his newfound strength and challenges him to confront the pain he may have ignored. The Dream Weaver's ominous warning hints at a deeper meaning behind Lloyd's journey, suggesting that there are still obstacles to overcome and truths to uncover. Will Lloyd be able to confront his past and embrace his inner turmoil, or will the darkness that threatens to engulf him will consume him? The answers lie within the depths of his own soul, waiting to be discovered amidst the shifting sands of the dreamscape.

Lloyd felt a wave of shame and sorrow crash over him, memories of times he had hurt others or turned away from those who needed him. This shadow-self carried the burden of every regret Lloyd had buried. "You can't run from me," it said. "I am as much a part of you as your light." The Dream Weaver stood silently, their glowing form fading, as if leaving Lloyd to face this new challenge alone. For the first time, Lloyd felt truly vulnerable. Anger, guilt, fear—they all surged within him. But as he looked into the eyes of his shadow, he realized the truth: his light had meaning only because of his darkness. They were two halves of the same whole. Gathering his courage, Lloyd spoke. "I see you," he said to the shadow. "You are my pain, my mistakes—but you've also taught me resilience, empathy, and strength. I don't fear you anymore."

In that moment of acceptance and self-awareness, Lloyd

understood the importance of embracing his shadow self. He recognized he should acknowledge and integrate his past mistakes and pain into his being, not shun or hide them. By acknowledging the darkness within him, Lloyd found a newfound sense of empowerment and wholeness. Lloyd's journey to self-acceptance and inner peace had begun. He was prepared for any challenges, embracing both his light and dark sides.

The shadow paused, its form flickering. Slowly, it stepped forward and merged with Lloyd, filling him with a profound sense of wholeness. The surrounding void collapsed, replaced by a serene, golden meadow. The Dream Weaver returned, their light more radiant than ever. "You've taken the ultimate step," they said. "The key to becoming who you are is embracing all that you are." The fog was gone, not just from his mind, but from his heart. And though he didn't know where his path would lead, he knew he was finally free to walk it fully, embracing every part of himself.

In this transformative moment, Lloyd experienced a profound merging of his shadow self with his conscious being, symbolizing a reconciliation of his inner conflicts and insecurities. The manifestation of a serene, golden meadow represents a newfound sense of inner peace and clarity. The wisdom imparted by the Dream Weaver underscores the importance of self-acceptance and embracing one's identity. This profound experience fills Lloyd with a deep sense of peace and liberation as he awakens. The metaphorical fog that once clouded his mind and heart has lifted, allowing him to see clearly and feel whole. With a newfound understanding of himself, Lloyd embraces every aspect of his being and embarks on a journey of self-discovery and personal growth.

We can view Lloyd's journey as a metaphor for the universal struggle of reconciling inner conflicts and insecurities. The merging of the shadow self with the conscious being represents a significant step towards wholeness and self-acceptance. The serene, golden meadow symbolizes a state of inner peace that comes from embracing all parts of oneself, even the darker aspects that were once hidden or suppressed.

The wisdom imparted by the Dream Weaver serves as a guiding light for Lloyd, reminding him of the importance of accepting himself fully and embracing his identity. This newfound clarity and understanding allow Lloyd to break free from the constraints of self-doubt and insecurity, paving the way for personal growth and transformation.

As Lloyd emerges from this transformative experience, a deep sense of peace and liberation fills him. The fog that once clouded his mind and heart has lifted, revealing a clear path forward. Lloyd, now self-aware and accepting, will embark on a journey of self-discovery. He's ready to explore himself and embrace his true self.

The narrative of Lloyd's journey serves as a powerful reminder of the transformative power of self-acceptance and embracing one's shadows. It highlights the importance of inner harmony and authenticity in unlocking one's true potential and finding a sense of fulfillment. Lloyd's story is a testament to the resilience of the human spirit and the capacity for growth and renewal that lies within each of us.

Long before Lloyd's journey, the Dream Weaver existed as a fragment of a long-forgotten constellation. They were born from the brightest star, which collapsed under the weight of unfulfilled dreams scattered across countless lives. These unspoken desires and forgotten hopes formed a powerful cosmic energy that lingered in the void. From this energy, the Dream Weaver emerged—a being with the unique purpose of mending fractured souls and guiding them through the labyrinth of their dreams.

The Weaver's realm existed beyond time and space, woven from the threads of every dream ever dreamed. They could hear the echo of every person's longing, fear, and hope, like a symphony of whispers. Yet, their origin was not without sorrow. The Dream Weaver was bound to their task, unable to leave their ethereal plane or experience the dreams they helped others confront. This solitude, however, granted them wisdom—a deep understanding of the human soul that only a being unshackled from mortal life could possess.

Cosmic energy from unfulfilled dreams intertwined with the Dream Weaver's existence, making them a guardian of lost hopes and aspirations. Their purpose was to mend the broken spirits of individuals by guiding them through the complexities of their subconscious minds. While they could not partake in the dreams themselves, the Dream Weaver's unique vantage point allowed them to gain profound insights into the human psyche.

In conclusion, the Dream Weaver stood as a beacon of compassion and wisdom, offering solace to those in need of healing and guidance within the vast tapestry of dreams. Over millennia, the Dream Weaver learned to adapt their form to each traveler they guided. A shimmering warrior appeared to the brave. To the lost, they became a beacon of light. To Lloyd, burdened by doubt and fear, they became a calm and steady presence, cloaked in gossamer starlight.

But beneath their serene exterior, the Dream Weaver harbored a secret: they too had a dream—a single, unfulfilled longing to understand what it meant to feel human. Every time they guided a traveler like Lloyd, they experienced humanity through the traveler's eyes—its beauty, its sorrow, and its triumphs. They carried glimpses of these emotions in their hearts. These glimpses, though never fully understood, formed a mosaic of what it meant to truly live.

The Dream Weaver's ability to empathize with and guide travelers through the realm of dreams was a testament to their profound connection to the human experience. Despite their ethereal nature, the Dream Weaver longed to grasp the essence of human emotions and sensations that eluded them. This desire fueled their dedication to each traveler they encountered, as they sought to glean insights into the complexities of human existence.

Through their interactions with individuals like Lloyd, the Dream Weaver gained a deeper understanding of the multifaceted nature of humanity. They gained new insights into the human condition with each encounter, enriching their understanding of life. The joys and struggles they witnessed added layers to their comprehension of what it meant to be truly alive. As they continued to weave their way through the dreams of others, the Dream Weaver carried with them a growing sense of empathy and insight that transcended their otherworldly origins.

In dreams, the Dream Weaver was a steadfast guardian and seeker. They connected the ethereal and earthly, showing humanity's essence through their luminous presence.

# 23

# Anchored in the Words of Christim

I N MATTHEW 11:28–30, JESUS says, "Come unto me, all ye that labour and are heavy laden, and I will give you rest. Take my yoke upon you and learn of me; for I am meek and lowly in heart; and ye shall find rest unto your souls. For my yoke is easy, and my burden is light." This passage from the Bible highlights Jesus' invitation to those who are struggling and in need of comfort. It emphasizes the idea of finding peace and solace in turning to Him for support and guidance.

To find the solace and peace we all desperately need, it is important to prioritize self-care and emotional well-being. We can achieve this through practices such as meditation, mindfulness, and deep breathing exercises. Engaging in activities that bring joy and relaxation, such as spending time in nature, reading an enjoyable book, or listening to calming music, can also help in finding solace.

Seeking support from loved ones, friends, or a mental health professional can provide comfort and guidance during challenging times. You must create a safe and nurturing environment for yourself where you acknowledge and process feelings and emotions healthily. By incorporating these practices into our daily lives, we can cultivate a sense of inner peace and tranquility.

Finding inner peace and tranquility has been an age-old process that individuals have sought through various practices, such as meditation, mindfulness, yoga, and self-reflection. The journey to inner peace often involves connecting with oneself on a deeper level, understanding one's emotions and thoughts, and learning to let go of stress and negativity. Many people also find solace in nature, art, music, and other forms of creative expression to cultivate inner peace. The quest for inner peace is a personal and ongoing journey that requires patience, self-awareness, and a commitment to self-care and well-being.

To connect with our inner being, it is important to practice self-reflection and mindfulness. You can achieve this through activities such as meditation, journaling, or spending time in nature. By tuning into our thoughts and emotions, we can better understand ourselves and our genuine desires. Connecting with our inner being requires us to listen to our intuition and trust our inner wisdom. It is a journey of self-discovery and self-acceptance that can lead to a deeper sense of fulfillment and peace.

In this profound message, Jesus invites those who are feeling exhausted and overwhelmed by life's challenges. He offers a promise of rest and relief to all who seek solace in Him. By taking on His yoke and learning from His example of gentleness and humility, we can find a sense of peace and rejuvenation for our weary souls. The burden that Christ offers us is not heavy but light, providing us with the strength and comfort needed to navigate life's trials with grace and resilience. We can find our anchor in these words of encouragement and hope.

There are many things in our daily lives that can weigh us down and leave us feeling exhausted and overwhelmed. From work deadlines and financial pressures to relationship struggles and health concerns, it's easy to become weary and burdened by the challenges we face. However, it's important to remember that we are not alone in these struggles and that there are ways to find support and relief. By acknowledging and addressing the sources of our stress and seeking help when needed, we can work towards lightening the load and finding greater peace and balance in our lives.

**Anchoring Our Faith in Christ's Words**

In times of uncertainty and turmoil, it is essential to ground our faith in the teachings of Christ. His words serve as a guiding light, offering solace and reassurance to those who believe in Him. By anchoring our faith firmly in His wisdom, we can find comfort and strength in knowing that He will provide everything necessary for our mental, spiritual, and physical well-being. Let us hold fast to these words of hope and trust in the divine guidance of Christ.

# 24

# The Anchors of Redemption and Justification

# Romans 3:23-24

ROMANS 3:23-24 GIVES US insights into the universal need for salvation and the grace of God.

"For all have sinned, and come short of the glory of God; Being justified freely by his grace through the redemption that is in Christ Jesus."

In these verses, the apostle Paul highlights the fact that all have sinned and fallen short of the glory of God. This emphasizes the commonality of humanity's sinful nature and the need for redemption. However, the passage also points to the gift of God's grace, which is freely given through Jesus Christ. This gift of grace provides a way for all to be justified and made right with God, regardless of their past sins. Romans 3:23-24 serves as a reminder of the inclusive nature of God's love and the offer of salvation available to all who believe.

We can best explain the glory of God as the radiant display of His divine attributes and majesty. It encompasses the awe-inspiring beauty, power, and holiness that are inherent in His nature. God's greatness and goodness overwhelm us when we experience His glory, filling us with reverence and worship. It is a profound and transformative encounter that reveals God's infinite love and sovereign rule over all creation. We come to know God's glory through His word, creation, and the Holy Spirit's work in our lives, even though it is beyond human comprehension. Seeking to understand and reflect His glory draws us closer to Him, and we find purpose and fulfillment living out His will.

**Phenomenon of Sin**

Sin is a complex and multifaceted phenomenon that has been a topic of discussion and debate for centuries. People commonly understand it as a violation of religious or moral laws, often harming oneself or others.

The concept of sin varies across different belief systems and cultures, with interpretations ranging from individual transgressions against divine commandments to broader societal injustices. The consequences of sin can be spiritual, emotional, or material and may manifest in feelings of guilt, shame, or alienation. Understanding the nature and implications of sin is a fundamental aspect of many religious and ethical traditions, shaping beliefs about morality, redemption, and human nature.

Various belief systems view sin as a transgression or violation of divine law or moral principles. This separation from the divine, or disruption of harmony between individuals and the spiritual realm, often makes up sin. Different religions and philosophies have varying perspectives on sin, with some emphasizing the need for repentance and atonement, while others focus on the importance of self-awareness and personal growth. The concept of sin plays a significant role in shaping individual ethics and guiding moral behavior in diverse cultures and traditions.

The origin of sin is a complex and multifaceted concept that theologians, philosophers, and scholars have explored throughout history. In Christianity, theologians often trace the origin of sin to the story of Adam and Eve in the Garden of Eden, where they disobeyed God's command. This disobedience, known as original sin, caused humanity's fall, and introduced sin into the world. However, different religious traditions and belief systems may have varying interpretations of how sin originated and its implications for humanity. Philosophical discussions on sin also delve into questions of free will, moral responsibility, and the human condition. Overall, the origin of sin is a complex and deeply ingrained concept that continues to be a subject of contemplation and debate.

## "Free Will"

The concept of free will posits that individuals possess the power of choice, unaffected by predetermined factors like fate. A discussion would explore this philosophical idea. This concept raises questions about human agency, the extent of our control over our actions, and the potential implications for moral responsibility and personal autonomy.

Philosophers, theologians, and scientists have debated the existence and implications of free will for centuries, exploring how it relates to determinism, causality, consciousness, and ethics. The discussion of free will delves into fundamental aspects of human nature and the complexity of decision-making processes.

"All have sinned" implies that every individual has committed wrongful acts or behaved in a way that goes against moral or ethical standards. Religious contexts often use this phrase to convey the belief that all humans are inherently flawed and have fallen short of perfection. It emphasizes the universal nature of human imperfection and the need for forgiveness or redemption.

## The Significance of Free Will in Accepting Christ's Sacrifice

In Christian theology, the concept of free will plays a crucial role in the acceptance of Christ's sacrifice on the cross for the remission of sin. The belief is that through our free will, we can choose to accept or reject the act of Christ's death as an atonement for our sins. This acceptance is a personal decision that everyone must make, acknowledging the importance of personal agency in matters of faith and salvation.

Christ's sacrifice manifests divine love and grace; by accepting it, individuals commit to their faith and desire forgiveness and redemption. Christians view the free choice to accept Christ's sacrifice as a core tenet of their faith, highlighting believers' personal accountability and independence in their relationship with God.

## "Justification by Faith"

In the study of theology and Christian doctrine, one of

the fundamental concepts that is often discussed is justification by faith. This concept highlights that salvation comes through faith in Jesus Christ alone, not through works or deeds. The Bible, especially the letters of Paul, grounds the concept of justification by faith. It is a central tenet of Protestant theology and has been a point of theological debate and discussion throughout the history of Christianity. This doctrine emphasizes that faith is how individuals reconcile with God and receive eternal life.

In the Catholic tradition, the concept of justification is a central theological idea that concerns the process by which a person is righteous in the eyes of God. Justification is a key aspect of salvation and grace, God's free and unmerited gift of love and forgiveness, intricately linked to it.

According to Catholic teaching, justification involves both God's initiative in offering grace and the individual's response to faith and good works. The Catholic Church emphasizes the importance of both faith and works in the process of justification, viewing them as complementary rather than opposing elements. This understanding of justification has been a point of theological debate and discussion within the broader Christian tradition.

In various world religions, the concept of justification

plays a significant role in shaping beliefs and practices. For example, in Christianity, justification is often associated with being made right with God through faith in Jesus Christ. In Islam, the weighing of a person's deeds on Judgment Day determines their salvation. Hinduism emphasizes the concept of karma, where one's actions and intentions in this life will determine their fate in future lives. Buddhism also incorporates the idea of justification through the concept of karma, with the belief that one's actions will have consequences in this life and future reincarnations. Overall, the concept of justification is a common thread in many world religions, influencing the beliefs and practices of followers.

**Overview of Redemption**

Finally, we take an overview of what redemption is. Redemption is a fundamental concept in various aspects of life, including finance, religion, and storytelling. In financial terms, redemption refers to the process of repurchasing or buying back securities or assets. This can involve redeeming bonds, shares, or mutual fund units at their face value or market price. In religious contexts, redemption often symbolizes the act of saving or delivering individuals from sin or evil, offering them the chance for forgiveness and spiritual renewal. In literature and film, redemption is a common theme where characters seek to atone for past mistakes or find personal salvation through acts of courage, sacrifice, or selflessness. Overall, the concept of redemption embodies the idea of transformation, growth, and the possibility of a fresh start in the face of adversity or wrongdoing.

Therefore, Romans 3:23-24 is an important verse for one's forgiveness and redemption, which anchors us in the word of God.

# 25

# The Anchor of Childhood

I N THE TENDER DAYS of my youth, my family dwelled in modesty, blissfully unaware of our financial plight. I did not understand our true financial circumstances until I began my studies. We rarely bought pencils, even though they cost almost nothing. My mother would impress upon us the importance of honing our existing pencils to the very eraser, a ritual that must precede any funds for a new pencil.

My classmates always had shiny, fresh supplies; their pencil cases filled with an array of colorful options. I remember feeling a twinge of envy, but also a sense of pride in making what we had last. My mom had a way of turning these minor challenges into lessons of resourcefulness and gratitude.

In those days, I remember how I would pick up pecans

from beneath our three trees to secure enough money to buy Christmas gifts. Each year, our school class would draw names, and the cheapest gift I could find was a box of chocolate-covered cherries. They were only fifty cents a box. That's the gift I would give each year to the person whose name I had drawn.

Despite our lack of possessions, love and laughter filled our home. My siblings and I spent countless hours playing outside, inventing games with whatever we could find. We turned sticks into swords, leaves into treasure maps, and our backyard into an imaginary kingdom.

Looking back, those days taught me the value of creativity and the importance of cherishing the simple joys in life. This perspective stays with me; I remind myself that happiness comes from family warmth and rich shared experiences, not material things.

As I grew older, I realized that those humble beginnings were the foundation of my resilience and adaptability. Each improvised game, each moment of inventive play, was a lesson in finding beauty in the ordinary. These experiences instilled in me a deep appreciation for the intangible gifts life offers—friendship, imagination, and the unwavering support of loved ones.

Even now, when I face challenges, I draw strength from those childhood memories. They remind me that obstacles can be opportunities in disguise and that true wealth lies in the connections we nurture and the memories we create. In a world that often equates success with accumulation, I'm grateful for the grounding lessons of my youth. They have shaped me into someone who finds joy in simplicity and who values the profound over the superficial. Life's richness lies in simple moments with family and creative pursuits. Remaining open to these experiences is key.

I vividly remember that summer when I was thirteen, as my father found himself hospitalized for three months, leaving our family to navigate the tides of survival. With the sun gleaming, our garden became a treasure trove of fresh vegetables to sustain us. Beyond that bounty, we sought the aid of the U.S.D.A. for essential staples to fill our table. Though the days were fraught with challenges, we persevered, bolstered by the grace of God.

Our community rallied around us, offering support in small yet meaningful ways. Neighbors would drop by with a casserole or freshly baked bread, their kindness a testament to the bonds that tie us all together. Resourcefully, my mother taught us to stretch our meals at the kitchen table and to be grateful for our food.

During those long summer days, I learned the true meaning of resilience. My siblings and I took on additional responsibilities, working together to maintain the household while my father recovered. We discovered strength in unity, each of us playing a vital role in keeping our family afloat.

Despite the hardships, there were moments of joy and laughter. We found solace in storytelling, sharing tales of our dreams and aspirations, our hopes of painting a brighter future. Those stories carried us through the toughest times, reminding us of the power of imagination and the promise of better days ahead. Although my dream was to become a doctor, I knew that my family could never support me through college or medical school, but I could dream. Isn't it ironic that I did eventually become a doctor? A Doctor of Theology!

As the summer faded into fall, my father returned home, his presence a beacon of hope. Though we faced many more challenges, the lessons we learned during those months were invaluable. They taught us that courage is born from adversity, and that love can light the darkest paths.

Looking back, I realize those experiences were not merely trials to endure, but opportunities to grow. They shaped our family, deepening our connections and fortifying our spirits. Even now, in moments of difficulty, I remind myself of that summer and the strength we found in each other. We can overcome any obstacle with resilience and love.

I carry those lessons with me, a constant source of inspiration and hope. They guide me through life's unpredictability, showing me that no challenge is insurmountable when faced with courage and unity. Whenever I find myself weighed down by the complexities of adulthood, I think back to those simpler times, where the power of family and community triumphed over adversity.

In sharing this story, I hope to pass on the wisdom of those days to others. Let us find comfort in our interconnectedness. Overcoming obstacles reveals both our inner resilience and the strength of our community. Let us cherish the love that sustains us and the memories that define us and let them be the compass that guides us through life's journey. These memories become an anchor for the soul.

# 26

# Contemporary Parables as Anchors

C ONTEMPORARY PARABLES THAT CONVEY time-less biblical truths in relatable ways beg us to learn more. These stories often hold a mirror to our own lives, encouraging introspection and growth. They weave ancient wisdom into modern narratives, offering fresh perspectives on age-old lessons about love, forgiveness, humility, and hope. Each parable, whether about a returning prodigal child or a transformative act of kindness, reminds us of faith's power and the importance of integrity and compassion. This is especially relevant in today's world. By connecting the past with the present, these tales invite us to reflect on our values and inspire us to act with grace and empathy in our everyday lives.

In a world that often feels disconnected and fast-paced,

these contemporary parables serve as anchors, grounding us in the enduring principles that guide a life well-lived. They remind us that, while the context and characters may change, the core messages remain relevant and urgent. As we navigate our own challenges, these stories offer comfort and guidance, illuminating paths of reconciliation, understanding, and courage.

These narratives encourage us to view our struggles not as insurmountable obstacles but as opportunities for transformation and growth. They inspire us to seek the beauty in the mundane and to find strength in vulnerability. These tales offer valuable lessons. By learning from them, we can better navigate the complexities of modern life with hope and a willingness to embrace change.

Contemporary parables remind us we are all part of a larger story, connected by timeless truths and shared human experiences. They invite us to be active participants in this story, shaping the world with acts of kindness, understanding, and love. Each narrative invites us to reflect on our own role in the unfolding drama of life, urging us to contribute positively to the tapestry of humanity. These stories challenge us to look beyond the surface, to delve deeper into the essence of what it means to live authentically and with purpose. They encourage us to listen more intently, to empathize more fully, and to engage with others compassionately, fostering a sense of community and belonging.

In embracing these teachings, we find the courage to rewrite our narratives and to be the change we wish to see in the world. Let's carry the lessons of these parables in our hearts. These parables should guide our actions and inspire us to create a more compassionate, understanding, and hopeful world.

Read the parables taught by Jesus again for reflection and meditation. See how revealing they are to our contemporary ways of living. They offer timeless wisdom that transcends the centuries, illuminating paths of righteousness and compassion. In these stories, we find profound insights that resonate with our current experiences, encouraging us to pause and reconsider our priorities and actions. The parables, using vivid imagery and interesting narratives, invite inward reflection. They challenge our assumptions and encourage a deeper understanding of the divine.

As we immerse ourselves in these teachings, we discover the enduring relevance of the values they espouse—love, mercy, humility, and justice. The tales of the Good Samaritan and the Mustard Seed inspire hope and faith. Both stories encourage kindness and remind us of the power of small actions. By embracing their lessons, we find the strength to navigate the complexities of modern life with grace and integrity.

In reflecting on these parables, let us open our hearts to the transformative power they hold. May they inspire us to cultivate empathy, to act with compassion, and to seek peace in our interactions with others. As we strive to embody the teachings of Jesus in our daily lives, we contribute to a more connected, understanding, and harmonious world.

By internalizing these timeless lessons, we become agents of change, fostering environments where love and kindness flourish. Each moment offers an opportunity to practice what we have learned, to bridge divides, and to build communities rooted in mutual respect and care.

As we ponder these stories, let us also be mindful of the impact our actions have on those around us. By choosing to lead with empathy and understanding, we pave the way for others to do the same, creating ripples of positivity that extend far beyond our immediate circles. In this way, the essence of these parables lives on, not just in words but in the tangible difference we make in the lives of others.

In today's world, where acts of kindness and compassion are more needed than ever, it is essential to reflect on the timeless lessons exemplified by the Good Samaritan. By extending a helping hand to those in need, we not only show our faith, but also cultivate a spirit of kindness within ourselves. Through these actions, we can create a legacy of love and hope that transcends barriers of time and place. This legacy serves as a beacon of light, reminding us of the enduring power of compassion and grace in making a positive impact on the world. Let us continue to embody the virtues of the Good Samaritan and strive to be beacons of hope and love in our communities.

# Epilogue

I F YOU'VE ENJOYED THIS work, please tell others. It is truly a labor of love that I have written it. You may find a listing of my books for sale at the following web address:

**https://www.drcharlescravey.com**

I am continually drafting new books at a rapid pace, so please keep me in your daily prayers. God is good!

If you would like to be put on my email mailing list announcing the latest releases, send it to:

**drrev@msn.com**

www.ingramcontent.com/pod-product-compliance
Lightning Source LLC
LaVergne TN
LVHW091217080426
835509LV00009B/1041